Evangelism

Evangelism

Doing Justice
and Preaching Grace

Harvie M. Conn

P U B L I S H I N G
P.O. BOX 817 • PHILLIPSBURG • NEW JERSEY 08865-0817

Library of Congress Cataloging-in-Publication Data

Conn, Harvie M.
        Evangelism: doing justice and preaching grace / Harvie M. Conn.
            p.   cm.
        Originally published: Grand Rapids, Mich. : Zondervan Pub.
House, 1982.
        Includes bibliographical references.
        ISBN-10: 0-87552-206-8
        ISBN-13: 978-0-87552-206-7
        1. Evangelistic work. 2. Church and social problems. I. Title.
[BV3790.C595   1992]
269'.2—dc20
                                                            92-15398

to Max and Margaret Diedrich

Contents

Preface

This book is not intended as a simple how-to-do-it manual on evangelism as traditionally known. Many authors have written too well on this topic for one more to try. For readers seeking that kind of discussion, I commend the titles given in the Notes and the excellent work by C. John Miller, *Evangelism and Your Church* (Phillipsburg, N.J.: Presbyterian and Reformed, 1980).

Rather, this is an effort to look at the relation between evangelism and social questions as two sides of the same coin. *Holistic evangelism* has more recently been the term used to describe what I mean. Perhaps *Lordship evangelism* is easier to pronounce and understand. I want to speak of evangelism in context, of giving cups of cold water to the thirsty world, but giving them in the name of the Lord. I speak not of an easy truce between faith and works, nor even a partnership. All partners may be equal but too frequently some are more equal than others. No, our goal is an interdependence that guards the integrity of both components and sees them constantly interacting.

I have purposefully avoided entering for the most part into the discussions that now engage evangelical attention in such circles as those of the Lausanne Committee on World Evangelization. Chapter 4 touches on the questions;

Evangelism: Doing Justice and Preaching Grace

but it is more splashing than bathing. I just want to say something positive and as practical as a seminary professor can get.

I have made very free use of materials appearing in periodical sources. I am grateful for those publishers who have given me permission to use my earlier writings. Chapter 1 is a development of "The Church's Mission to All the Lost," published in the *Reformed Review* 32 (Spring 1979): 141–49. Chapter 4 draws from "Can I Be Spiritual and at the Same Time Human?" which appeared in *The Other Side* (September–October 1973), pp. 16–19, 42–47. A great portion of chapter 5 was originally published as "Luke's Theology of Prayer" in *Christianity Today* (22 December 1972), pp. 6–8. Chapter 6 is based on "Models of Ministry for the 1980s," which was published in the *Journal of Pastoral Practice* 3, no. 3 (1979): 109–120. I also express my appreciation to the Glenmary Research Center, Washington, D.C., for permission to make extensive use of the study by J. Russell Hale, *Who Are the Unchurched? An Exploratory Study.*

My prayer is that this book will not emerge as one more exercise in blackboard evangelism, one more illegitimate way of providing both writer and reader with one more excuse to learn a little bit more and do a little bit less, to keep off the streets and out of the kitchens. One prominent American cleric was supposed to have said once to the New York State Legislature: "I'm not going to pray for you. There are certain things a man does for himself. He has to blow his own nose, make his own love, and say his own prayers." To the list I add, do his own witnessing. And now to the streets and not, pray God, to the study.

1

Can the Church Be All Things to All People?

Christ's church is in trouble. By the end of 1978, the United Presbyterian Church in the USA had lost that year forty-seven thousand members. In the Episcopal Church, membership losses have been so sharp that it has been estimated that if present trends continue there will be one priest for each communicant by the year 2000.[1] Presumably, these losses have contributed to the estimated eighty million unchurched Americans, roughly 40 percent of the population, the subject of a recent study by J. Russell Hale.[2]

The real jolt in these figures may be the reasons for church dropouts. According to George Gallup, the unchurched are not giving up Billy Graham for Madeline Murray O'Hare. Gallup's 1978 study, *The Unchurched American,* indicates that 68 percent of the unchurched believe in the resurrection of Christ, 64 percent believe Christ is God or the Son of God, and 70 percent read the Bible.

Then why the decline? According to the pollster, 60 percent of the unchurched believe that "most churches and synagogues have lost the real spiritual part of religion." About half agree that "most churches and synagogues today are not effective in helping people find meaning in life." It seems that a large percentage of the unchurched do not believe the church can be all things to all people. The church's theme song has become, "Put a little love away, save it for a rainy day." Are we too much like warehouses or amusement parks? And too little like U-Haul trucks, "an adventure in moving"?

A Theology of Scratching Where People Itch

The "in" word we must pay attention to is *contextualization*, the art of planting the gospel seed in culture's diverse soils without also planting the flower pot. Mortimer Arias, a Bolivian Methodist, calls it "contextual evangelism." It is the kingdom vision of Immanuel, God with us. It puts special emphasis on that "with us." If Christ is the answer, what are the real questions? Does God speak my language? How can we live out and share the gospel without domesticating the new wine?

I am not talking simply about the relevance of the gospel. I am talking about how to communicate the relevance of the gospel. How really telling is our telling?

Ordinarily western theological seminaries do not help us in answering this question. Communication is oriented toward the insider, not the outsider. We ask churchy questions, we learn a churchy vocabulary—redemption, sin, grace, eschatology. Our Bible translations meet the same standards. Are they "faithful" or are they "paraphrases"? New International Version brand? Or Good News Bible type? Are they suitable for "reading in worship"? Behind all the questions is the hidden agenda of our target audience: Christian or non-Christian? Ministerial skills assume that communication is a one-way process, the technique of passing on our message (assumed to be God's) from the communicator to the receptor. Homiletics trains us in the skills of gift-wrapping the package. Exegesis trains us in the art of gift selection. Church history tells us what hasn't worked, apologetics tells us what should. And all this time the seminary reinforces this one-way direction by providing a living model for the process. The institution is gift-oriented, not gift-receiver or gift-giver oriented. The schooling model reinforces a pattern for communication where effectiveness is largely measured in terms of the digestion of prepackaged packets of information—information aimed largely at a white Anglo-Saxon receptor. Then, ten years later at an alumni gathering, we wonder why our churches look white and Anglo-Saxon and suburban.

Missing in all of this is a Pauline sense of solidarity with a wide ethnic spectrum of hearers (1 Cor. 9:19–23). When Paul says, "I have become all things to all men, so that by all possible means I might save some," he is not engaged in gospel modification, homiletical cutting and paring. He is "under orders" to the changeless gospel (9:16). But it is precisely this changelessness that liberates him to change in terms of the life-situation of his hearers. He is not talking about the mere act of adjustment, proposing one more curriculum for one more Successful Church Seminar. In the light of the coming of the kingdom, he is exhorting us to circumcise our half-Jewish Timothys (Acts 16:3), to take our temple vows (Acts 18:18), to participate in our purification ceremonies for suburban Nazirites (Acts 21:17–26). His focus, and ours, is not on the technique of adjustment but on the demands created by the "now" of the kingdom.

This attention to the receptor is nothing new. It is rooted in the very nature of God the Father as the ultimate communicator. God, in seeking to reveal Himself to us, does so within the human frame of reference. Theologians call this *anthropomorphism*—God lisping that we might hear and understand, lowering Himself to the level of baby talk (Heb. 1:1–2). God's omnipotence becomes the arm of the Lord, his omniscience the eye of the Lord, His mercy portrayed as God repenting.

On a larger scale, the same process is described by others as biblical theology, what Geerhardus Vos has called the history of special revelation. Revelation has a history, unfolded in installments, of which each is divinely adapted to the ability of Adam and his sons and daughters to understand. The revelation of God does not burst the bonds of creation; it mediates itself to the cosmos through man's consciousness. Revelation has a history because God respects our creaturely existence. Revelation honors it without capitulating to it, adjusts to it without compromising its own truth-filled character. It bends down without being distorted.

The supreme revelation of the Father's will is in the Son, Jesus Christ. God did not shout His message down from heaven or from across the Jordan River. He entered our sphere, our environment, our cosmos. The Logos of God became flesh. In contrast, the Jewish parties of Jesus' day retreated from this incarnational model of communication. The Pharisees argued that sacred forms are more important than the fleshing out of the gospel in the Son. The Sadducees saw worldly sophistication and political power as more important than the incarnate power of the kingdom of God. The Essenes exalted separatism and militancy. Jesus broke through these stereotypes by becoming flesh. He interacted with human beings in their frame of reference. He learned to sympathize with human beings by allowing Himself to be subjected to their temptations and sufferings (Heb. 2:10, 17, 18; 4:15; 5:8).

Even the work of the Holy Spirit is audience-oriented. As culture builders and organizers, we build screens and create models of reality that filter the world to us. Anthropologists and ethnologists spend lifetimes studying the way our view of culture, our world view, structures reality for us. Our eyeglasses are self-constructed preferences, biases, predispositions toward God, man, and the world. We see what we want to see.

At the center of the filtering process is a heart in rebellion against God. Many Americans, therefore, filter out of their perception of reality any idea of the supernatural. The miraculous is a category left for Ripley's *Believe It or Not.* They read *The Hiding Place* and see it as the story of a woman with high ideals who showed remarkable resiliency under pressure, aided by her religious faith. They do not see the triumph of grace in the life of Corrie Ten Boom. They are skeptical of the conversion of Charles Colson, even more so of Larry Flynt and Eldridge Cleaver. And when these people goof, they sneer "We told you so." Their grid is preprogramed to reject the possibility of genuineness in Christian testimony.

Given this human process of model building and perceptualization, how can unbelievers genuinely see? How can they perceive reality as it is, when what they discover depends on what they are looking for, the questions they are asking, and the answers they already are suggesting? How can they be kept from constantly twisting the revelation of God until it becomes merely a projection onto their experience? If one's world view is constructed by one's religious commitment and by a culturally conditioned perception of reality, how can communication of the gospel ever be possible?

The answer to these questions is the work of the Holy Spirit. Through inspiration, the Spirit secures the Scriptures for the church. Because of the work of the Spirit, we may trust their verbal form as an adequate, authentic, and sufficient vehicle of special revelation. The integrity of the Bible is not blurred by the cultural settings the Spirit was pleased to use.

As the Illuminator, the Holy Spirit is person-oriented. What Berkeley Mickelsen calls "actualization" takes place: A past event becomes contemporary for a generation removed in space and time from the original event and from its cultural setting.[3] The Holy Spirit repersonalizes the Bible across different world views. In the process, the world view of the receptor begins to change at its core The illumination of the Spirit redemptively carries the message of the Bible from source to receptor without distorting its saving impact. The cultural foolishness of the Cross to the Greek becomes the wisdom of God (1 Cor. 1:18). The cultural stumbling block of the Cross to the Jew becomes the salvation of God (1 Cor. 1:23).

God scratches where the world itches; He accommodates His revelation to the agenda set by the world. But that agenda never overpowers the message of His kingdom. Addressed to one audience, it is the message of the "kingdom of heaven" (Matt. 4:17). Addressed to another, it is the message of the "kingdom of God" (Mark 1:15). Addressed to still another, "preaching the kingdom of God" is reencoded to "teaching concerning the Lord Jesus Christ" (Acts 28:23, 31).

The Art of Itch Discernment

Recognizing the importance of our audience, can we develop a genuine sensitivity to the needs of people without drifting toward a Madison Avenue philosophy of public relations? Will God become only our "great felt-need-meeter" in the sky? Can we develop a concern for itches without catering to people with "itching ears" (2 Tim. 4:3)? I think we can if we take into consideration the following points.

Is Our Message Cultural or Demythologized?

Missionaries in the past decade have been repeatedly warned against promoting what some call culture Christianity, the mixing of cultural givens with the gospel. A 1978 Lausanne-sponsored Consultation on Gospel and Culture warned: "Where missionaries bring with them foreign ways of thinking and behaviour, or attitudes of racial superiority, paternalism or preoccupation with material things, effective communication will be precluded."[4]

But one does not have to cross a culture to acknowledge this problem: it affects us right here at home. Loaded with our cultural baggage, how can we communicate the gospel without paying for excess weight? May I suggest that we begin with a recognition that our message needs biblical (not Bultmannian) demythologizing; it needs freedom from the cultural values and attitudes that hinder its effective communication. Loaded with his own mythical baggage, will the real evangelical please stand up and tell the truth?

Racism is a part of the mythology that inhibits our message. Not the white-hooded kind that burns crosses on lawns, but the sophisticated variety that runs in culture shock from a "changing" neighborhood to the mission-compound security of the suburbs. A former GI moves from Albuquerque to southern California and drops out of the church. "Manuel had a conflict there," his wife shares. "He is Mexican-American. That didn't seem to make any difference in Albuquerque, but it does here. Certain remarks were made by certain people. He won't go to that church again." A former government official, now living in Florida, speaks of a similar experience: "One of my good friends—he is the principal financial supporter of the Methodist church over here—continues to tell nigger stories. He won't have a black man to dinner for all the tea in China."

Preoccupation with money matters, the affluency myth, also affects us as we measure the mission of the church in terms of dollars and cents. This is why it is easier to solicit funds in the church for a building than for a 20 percent increase in benevolence giving. Meetings of congregations and church leaders are often dominated by questions of budget and property. It is the tether that ties us to the security of building in a new "model community" instead of the risk of the inner city. It is mirrored in the voice of a United Way executive in California, disillusioned after her long previous leadership and involvement in national church agencies: "I think the churches have gotten like a lot of parts of society. They have to worry so much about paying the rent that they have forgotten the good news. They forget the evangelical message."

Another example of cultural baggage is the expertise myth. It measures gifts of the Spirit in terms of formal schooling, scheduling, and planning ministry in unilateral terms of what has worked for "us." "Others" are invited to join in on our terms and frequently at a later stage. The myth ties us to structures and methods that have worked in the past but may not be working now. Coupled with our orientation toward dollars and cents, this myth can turn the helpful insights of the church-growth movement into a socio-theological defense of success at the expense of people. The "poor" to whom the gospel is basically committed are spiritualized by our pulpits into the "humble-minded." And the "locked-out" of our cities once more become invisible to the visible church.

"Privatization" also hinders our witness. Recent research underlines the growing power of the privatization myth of the evangelical. Built out of the American model of the rugged individual, it reduces sin's social dimensions to individual sins, and compartmentalizes our lives into dichotomies—sacred and secular, private and public sectors, stay-in and stay-out zones. It is reflected in the Gallup poll that found that 76 percent of those who go to church (and 86 percent of the unchurched) agree that "an individual should arrive at his or her own religious beliefs independent of any churches or synagogues." Privatization slips quickly into anti-institutionalism. It is, affirms Leighton Ford, an issue that needs to be confronted head-on—"the desire to have freedom to decide for ourselves and not to have anyone else tell us what to believe or not." We must face what Carl S. Dudley calls the new believer—those who have beliefs that parallel those of the church people but, as a result of the church's failure to struggle with privatization, move in the direction of greater individualism, personal freedom, tolerance of diversity, and distance from many traditional institutions.[5] Our unpaid bills have become our creditors.

Is Our Church the Message as Well as the Medium?

The message of the Gospels is that we no longer look for the reign of God through a telescope. We open our eyes to see it directly. What we see is Jesus and the firstfruits of the final harvest day. We see the church witnessing to the kingdom come in Christ and coming in Christ; it is a news reporter for the kingdom. But we also see the church as an instrument of the kingdom and as part of the good news of the kingdom. The keys of the kingdom are not locked in a drawer. They are given to the church (Matt. 16:18–19). The kingdom is not the possession of the church; the church is part of the kingdom treasure we possess, not just evangelistic machinery, but part of the package we call the good news. It has been placed on the earth to proclaim the kingdom and to exemplify it.

This has not always been our practice. The church as institution has slipped by practice into the church as technology. Our North American technological mentality has reshaped the church; program maintenance has become our primary goal. The success orientation of technocracy cranks out programs and activities. The smoothly functioning machine's resistance to change minimizes the prophetic function of the church to society. Bigness has become a sign of greatness, professionalism a sign of leadership, decision-making power the gloved fist of clerical administration. In the process, communication becomes verbalization, the passing of 11:00 A.M. Sunday memos from the administration to the volunteer staff. The church's value has become measured in terms of advertising copy, not in terms of a "letter . . . known and read by everybody" (2 Cor. 3:2). Church growth is translated into church duplicating; foot washing for society has become ecclesiastical cloning.

How will such a church minister to the growing wave of "anti-institutionalists" described by Gallup and the studies of Russell Hale? Or what of those Hale describes as "the locked-out"? A prisoner in a Boone County jail said, "The church is the kind of place where you get hit over the head, not loved. . . . I don't think very much of them."

What message has the church delivered to the social worker in Liberty, Maine who commented: "It is nice to have the sweet little old lady with white hair who smells of lavender in one of the middle-class or upper-class churches, but if you get someone from the hills who smells, they don't want her around."

Is Our Strategy Preacher-oriented or People-oriented?

How much of our gospel communication is determined by what the preacher or the theological professor thinks we need, rather than by the concrete needs of people? David's sin of adultery and murder was not confessed until a prophet sent by God touched the king's sense of justice. In response

Evangelism: Doing Justice and Preaching Grace

to a parable David cried out in real anger, "As surely as the LORD lives, the man who did this deserves to die!" (2 Sam. 12:5). Then came the word that brought change: "You are the man!" (12:7). Our Lord probed the life of a Samaritan woman at the well. When he touched the part of her life where she sensed need, her heart responded to His messianic claim. God never speaks in the abstract, but always to real people with real needs. And always in response to those needs. The covenant promise to a childless Abraham was not delivered as an abstract universal principle. It was couched in the concrete language of descendants who, like stars and sand, would be innumerable.

How does one discern felt needs? Hale's study reveals the unsecret secret: we must learn to really listen. He says, "The overwhelming experience my conversations with the unchurched conveyed to me was that those outside the churches want and need to be heard. . . . The vast majority, when they sensed that I was honestly open to hear even the most insignificant (to me) or ridiculous (to them) or poignant (to anyone who listens) of autobiographical episodes, related what I can only judge to have been authentic stories."[6]

Dietrich Bonhoeffer puts it this way: "The first service that one owes to others . . . consists in listening to them. . . . Many people are looking for an ear that will listen. They do not find it among Christians, because these Christians are talking when they should be listening. . . . Christians have forgotten that the ministry of listening has been committed to them by Him who is Himself the great listener and whose work they would share. We should listen with the ears of God that we may speak the Word of God."[7]

Does our model of evangelism as talking inhibit the obligations of evangelism as hearing? Does our failure to listen help create Hale's category of the boxed-in—those who feel constrained, or thwarted or kept from full independence and freedom by the churches? Is this why a pastor in southern California left the ministry? "I couldn't talk to the bishop or church people," he told Hale. "There were other people outside the church who were much more open. People in

20

the church, well, I got a lot of judgment. . . . So I went to outside people, outside of the church. And I found much more acceptance, much more affirmation of me as a human being." Can we translate openness and affirmation as "listening"?

Where do we go to listen? Most of us cannot take a six-month sabbatical as Hale did. But there are shorter routes. We can listen when people are examined for church membership. We may ask, "What brought you to Christ?" or "Why did you remain outside the kingdom till now?" We can take our informal surveys at Rotary Club meetings, on Little League baseball diamonds, at neighborhood swimming pools, in hospital rooms, and in retirement homes.

Will the unchurched talk? Says Hale, "I am convinced, on the basis of my association with the unchurched in six counties, that the outsider will welcome the insider who will listen with patience. Almost without exception, my informants' last words were 'Thank you' or 'I wish I could talk more' or 'Please stay for lunch, or coffee or a glass of wine.' Many invited me back. Some gave me mementos of the visit. . . . Not a few said goodbye with a warm handclasp or a spontaneous embrace. Even the more hostile were anxious to convey appreciation for my accepting their anger."[8] Perhaps our door-to-door surveys have started with the wrong kinds of questions. Maybe it's time we stop asking, "Would you like to come to our church?" and begin constructing surveys around the sincere statement, "We'd really like to know why you're not going anywhere."

Is Our Approach Pastoral or Patent-medicinal?

Gospel communication may be either direct or indirect. It may use earthquakes in Philippian jails or "altars to an unknown god." But whether direct or indirect, it is people standing together before God. And, either way, it must be pastoral.

Such communication sees through a person's name, position, reasons, and arguments and tries to reach the real life's problems. It involves meetings, but meetings filled

Evangelism: Doing Justice and Preaching Grace

with love. We recognize ourselves in the other person. Daniels look at the sins of Israel and cry, "We have sinned against you" (Dan. 9:8). Missionaries are not annoyed by the "stupidity" of the "natives," at their "primitive" behavior. This personal involvement with others determines the pastoral dimension of our work. Bearing the balm of Gilead, and not patent medicine, we are motivated by the heart of the shepherd.

Would a pastoral approach win back Hale's category of the burned-out? The burned-out are those who feel that their energies have been utterly consumed by the church. They have known the inside, and it has depleted their resources, talents, and time. Among them are the used. The church had used up all they had to give but continued to expect more. Instead of pastoral concern, there had been pressure, and expectations had become exploitations.

Without a pastoral dimension the offense of the gospel too easily is understood as the offensiveness of the church. The unchurched have no perception of a loving God who accepts persons while they are yet sinners.

A brutal example of this was provided by the recent Hollywood film *Hard Core*, written and directed by a young man raised in an evangelical church. It is an agonizing experience for anyone from that community and the wider evangelical world to watch the film. The focus of the story is a lay member of the "Christian Reformation Church." His daughter has run away from home and joined the unchurched in the world of pornographic film. The hero goes to find her and recruits for the search a teen-age prostitute.

In a scene I think every gospel communicator should see, the hero, Jake, sits with the prostitute in an airport lobby waiting for the plane to take them to a California city and the conclusion of their search. Jake is reading a newspaper. The girl asks him about his church background. As nearly as I can remember the dialogue, it begins with a question from the girl: "What church do you go to?"

"Well, we're a Calvinistic church."

"Calvinistic? I don't understand."

"Well, we believe in the Canons of Dordt." There is a

look of confusion on her face. He continues, "You know, the five points of Calvinism: T-U-L-I-P."

"Tulip?" she asks.

"Yes, that's an acronym," he continues, still reading. "T stands for total depravity."

"Total depravity?"

"Yes, all men are totally unable to do any good. . . ." At this point the plane is announced, Jake puts down his paper, and they head for the door.

The most frightening part of that scene is not what Jake said with his verbal symbols. Sovereign grace is sovereign grace, no matter how you spell it. It was what he really conveyed to that teen-age prostitute, to a girl whose whole life was sex and brutality. He was talking about grace without talking grace. The Lord's sheer mercy had become an empty sign with faded letters.

And, beyond it all, I found myself asking, "Is the filmmaker trying to tell me why he left the church?" Will some sensitive Christian film critic assume a pastoral role and open some door of communication to him? Or had his hometown newspapers already thundered their rejections so loudly at him that he'll never hear God's grace notes?

Is Our Concern Parochial or Universal?

Ultimately this question sums up all the others. Certainly without a right answer to it, all the dangers we warn against become realities. For too long evangelical white Christian communities in the United States have had a "come" structure, a parochialism that identifies with saints. One cannot be a missionary church and continue insisting that the world must come to the church on the church's terms. It must become a "go" structure. And it can do that only when its concerns are directed outside itself toward the poor, the abused, and the oppressed. The church must recapture its identity as the only organization in the world that exists for the sake of its nonmembers.

The Mennonite missiologist Wilbert Shenk is right: "The church suffers from morphological fundamentalism. In simple language this means the church is unwilling to tinker with time-honored forms and organizations."[9] What will break it free? What will turn it again to the problems of the urban poor, problems not of meaninglessness but oppression, not hopelessness but injustice? Where will the American world turn for answers to great questions—our brutalized cities, our battered families, ethnic communities tired of hearing "suburban is beautiful," suburbanites rushing back to the cities to appease their guilt of neglect or to get a quicker, cheaper ride to work? What will break the church free?

The locked-out feel not wanted, excluded from the fellowship of churches they have known. The cop-outs have found worship services dull, repetitious, unexciting. The pilgrims want to question the church and have their questions answered. They fault the traditional, authoritarian "take it or leave it" style of Christian communication. The boxed-in react negatively to what they perceive to be the church's emphasis on submission. The publicans raise questions about the credibility of a church that, according to them, says one thing and does another. Can we speak to them again and this time be heard?

We will have to repent, to "turn around." When a Sister of Charity in Alabama heard the findings of Russell Hale that I have summarized in this chapter, she put it in a nutshell: "What we need to say to our unchurched brothers and sisters is, 'You are right in all your criticism of the churches. We ask your forgiveness.'" That can take place with a renewal of our missionary vision for the church, the abandonment of our ghetto parochialism. "We in the churches are being spied upon," said Jacques Ellul.

Will we respond with the voice of an Old Testament saint who was also spied upon? "The LORD your God is God in heaven above and on the earth below" (Josh. 2:11).

2

If Jesus Is the Answer, What Are the Questions?

Once upon a time, begins the parable drawn by Dr. Jack Miller of Westminster Seminary, there was a splendid fishing trawler docked at a seaport near some of the world's richest fishing grounds. The large boat was well equipped with everything necessary for netting, landing, and preserving fish. On a regular basis the officers and crew gathered for instruction in fishing theory. Afterwards they discussed with zeal and intelligence the various approaches to fishing. Sometimes they invited professors from the marine biology academy nearby to offer special lectures. Some maintained that the only way to fish was to anchor and pray that the Lord would send the fish into the nets. Few of these men attended the prayer meetings called for this purpose. Several argued for friendship fishing, noting that fish are easily frightened. Others held to the position that it is best to seek out the young ones, otherwise they will soon swim away into the deep.

In the meantime, day after day the other fishing boats went out early in the morning and returned at evening loaded with fish. The officers and crew often analyzed their catches. "Mostly culls, easy catches of surface fish," they said. "Their boats are not as sound as ours. Their nets leak and their engines are not kept up. Their refrigeration systems are bad, so that what they catch they can never keep long enough to get it to the cannery."

Yet the trawler remained tied to the dock with heavy lines. The engines never roared into life.

One day a critical young crew member was called before the captain and the crew. He had been critical of the continuing education program and very frustrated by the ship's inactivity. "We are one of fifteen ships in our line. Ten of our ships last year caught only twenty-nine fish. What is wrong?"

Questions were fired at him by the crew, and he responded even more boldly. "Why do we always sit here tied to the dock? Why do we study fishing theory without going out into the deep? Why do we watch others fish and never fish ourselves? I know other ships are not as well equipped as ours, but isn't what they do imperfectly better than what we don't do at all?"

Some wanted to fire the young man right on the spot. Others urged caution. After all, at one time the ship had put to sea and landed great catches of fish. Finally, a decision was made. A committee was selected to study the matter. That was five years ago. The committee is still studying. And there are rumors of at least two minority reports soon to be presented with a majority report. There are four men on the committee.[1]

Allegories are a little like tonsilectomies. It hurts only when we smile and swallow our medicine. Hopefully this one will in one important point be dissimilar to a tonsilectomy. Our purpose is not to aid in the removal of a growth but to cultivate growth.

How do we begin our search for a definition of evangelism? We have enough questions for a book the size of a Sears Roebuck catalog. What is the relation between missions and evangelism? Between evangelism and social action? Can you have Christian proclamation without presence, word without deed? Should we buy Peter Wagner's distinction between merely proclamation evangelism and his alternative choice, persuasion evangelism? Is ours a "theology of search" or a "theology of harvest"?

26

If Jesus Is the Answer, What Are the Questions?

We begin with a working definition supplied by John Knox: "Give me Scotland or I die." Evangelism is Henry Martyn landing on the shores of India and crying, "Here let me burn out for God!" It is George Whitefield crossing the Atlantic thirteen times in a small boat to preach in the American colonies. It is a testimony: "Once I was blind, now I see." It is a piece of gossip shared between brothers: "We have found the Messiah."

Others provide a more formal analysis. Jerald Gort suggests that evangelism is "the liberating coming of God in Christ through His disciples to people who no longer know or have never known him,"[2] Lesslie Newbigin calls it the "open secret, . . . proclaiming the kingdom of the Father, sharing the life of the Son, bearing the witness of the Spirit."[3] It is going into the world because He has come to the world. It is "proclaiming the past and present liberating work of Christ in such a way that people are led into the ongoing process of conversion and into communities of faith demonstrating and proclaiming the lordship of Christ." It is opening doors into treasure houses of the kingdom.[4] It is calling people to conversion, an eschatological journey, a pilgrimage to Christ, to culture, and to the world.[5]

Evangelism in Terms of What the World Needs

What brings North Americans into the fellowship of the good news? How does evangelism meet their needs? What are those needs? A 1972 sampling of 3,450 church members and pastors sought to find out what Christians in the North American continent thought about the church.

Evangelism as a Call to Reconciliation With God

In an era used to slogans like "post-Christian" and "crisis of faith," the data in the 1972 study showed that people, of all ages and categories, of much education and little, young and old, "strongly subscribe to the classically stated doctrines of Christianity. . . . These include belief in God as heavenly Father. . . . , in salvation from sin, in the Scrip-

Evangelism: Doing Justice and Preaching Grace

tures as the Word of God, in Jesus Christ as God's revelation to man, in Christ as a continuing living reality and in eternal life beyond death."[6] For all areas and groups, the cardinal concern of the church is seen as meditating on the message of Jesus, persuading others to believe and trust His unique authority and way. "The church must return to the preaching of the gospel," declared an Ohio salesman. "It is the only way we can be effective."

Hale's survey of 1977 reinforces this from another point of view. Those not on the rolls of the church, the unchurched, do not reject the church because it preaches "good news." They reject the church because they have been learning more "bad news" than "good news." "Sectarian versions of the Christian message have come across to many who are now outsiders as overloaded with law, moralism, judgment, and rejection. Many have simply never heard of a loving God who accepts persons while they are yet sinners. If the Christian gospel is an offense to the unbeliever, it is legitimate to ask whether the gospel has in reality been proclaimed and whether the offense may lie in the offensiveness of the proclaimers."[7]

What does the church perceive as the instrument of the good news? The 1972 survey offered a list of fourteen possible functions. "The paramount No. 1 task of the local church" was seen as "reaching beyond itself in evangelism —'winning others to Christ.'"[8] Midway in the list of choices was this function: "to serve as social conscience to the community." Lower down, in the bottom half of the list, came such things as providing "fellowship" and "facilities for activities" of members.

All of this simply means that evangelism does have a relation to the existential situation of humanity. "Evangelism is in the first place the transmission of God's question to man. And that question is and remains whether we are willing to accept Jesus Christ as the one and only Lord of life."[9] In answering God's question, men and women find at the same time the answer to their deepest concerns.

At the center of evangelism is a single word, God's good news—Jesus. When Philip sat down beside the Ethiopian, we are told that "he evangelized to him Jesus" (Acts 8:35, literal translation). This Jesus is not the lovable, innocent teacher of *Godspell* but "Lord both of the dead and of the living" (Rom. 14:19). Not the secular Jesus of radical theology but He who sealed His ministry by suffering and on the third day rising from the dead (Luke 24:44). Not the Jesus failure of the Moonies, pointing us to the need for a new messiah today, but the Jesus exalted by God "to his own right hand as Prince and Savior that he might give repentence and forgiveness of sins to Israel" (Acts 5:31).

Evangelism as a Call to Incorporation

Evangelism is God's answer to the needs of the boxed-in. Theirs is a search for genuine community, angry as they are with a church that constrains them and thwarts their potential for growth. An Oregon newspaper publisher draws boxes on newsprint. He labels each with an organizational title—the Rotary, the parish, the Fire Department. Outside all the boxes, he marks a heavy black dot. "That's me," he says. "I am on the outside. I go in when I need the in-group. . . . Boxes constrain me."[10]

There are also the locked-out. They feel the churches have closed their doors against them. A divorcee perceives herself as "not good enough." A black janitor sees himself as overlooked, "the invisible American." A young sculptor in California analyzes his church experiences. "Dead people going in," he says, "no life in them, sitting in pews, coming out. Rich people sit in the front, poor people sit in the back. Years of that makes you dried up. . . . They got their own little group, their own little people."[11]

Often for these unchurched groups, the neighborhood bar becomes the best substitute in meeting their need. Bruce Larson describes it this way: "It's an imitation, dispensing liquor instead of grace, escape rather than reality, but it is a permissive, accepting and inclusive fellowship. It is unshockable. It is democratic. You can tell people secrets and they usually don't tell others or even want to. The bar flourishes, not because most people are alcoholics, but because God has put into the human heart the desire to know

29

and be known, to love and be loved, and so many seek a counterfeit at the price of a few beers. . . ."[12] The bar becomes the point of contact for the singles, the communion rail for the homosexual.

At the center of evangelism should be an answer—the kingdom of God embodied in a community of salvation and sharing. Jesus' evangelism in the Nazareth synagogue is the announcement of the Jubilee year blessing—good news for society's leftovers, the etceteras of culture, the poor, the imprisoned, the blind, the downtrodden (Luke 4:18–21). For Peter evangelism is the demonstration of the church's service-in-love (1 Peter 1:22; 2:17; 3:8; 4:8–11). Paul's authenticity as an evangelist of the kingdom is proved by a collection for the Jerusalem poor (Gal. 2:9–10). The kingdom is evangelized by forming covenanted communities out of "sheep without a shepherd," out of the boxed-in and the locked-out. It is a community of identification—Jew with Gentile, slave with free, men with women. And the center around which they cluster is the one that is "in Christ" (Gal. 3:28). It is a community of acceptance and "one anothering"—"not passing judgment on one another" (Rom. 14:13), having "concern for one another" (1 Cor. 12:25), "bearing with one another in love" (Eph. 4:2), having overflowing love for one another" (1 Thess. 3:12). There is room for Oregon newspaper publishers and California sculptors.

Evangelism as a Call to Humanization

Evangelism speaks to the issues raised by the burned-out. The church, they argue, refuses them their humanity. They become objects to be used, instruments and not people. They suffer from an internal energy crisis, their resources, talents, and time depleted by an ecclesiastical Three Mile Island.

Within this category are the used, those who feel they have been exploited or manipulated. They are overworked church leaders who have dropped out; they wear a badge on their Florida retirement sport shirts—"too pooped to participate." Their reflections on church experience are studded with words like "too much," "overexposure as a child," "just got tired." A Methodist woman speaks for the group. "They kept saying, "If you come to church, why not every Sunday?' If you go every week, there's pressure for more involvement. I tried it for a while, but no more." A woman, active in community affairs in California, complains, "When they see a leader, they hook you. They say, 'Here is an executive. She's in our church—let's use her and make her do these things.' Before long, it's 'Will you teach Sunday school or will you do this, will you do that?' I really can't get involved. Once in a while, yes, but not just giving, giving, giving."[13]

Another type of the burned-out are the light travelers. In their past the church was important. They have no regrets. But now they have reached a stage in life when such baggage is optional. They want to travel more lightly late in life. An overnight bag will do. For the light traveler Florida and California are not geography. They are retirement states of mind. "This is a start-over state," one of them says. "Many of the people moving here are looking for a fresh start. Either they are severing their ties from back home or they are looking for the Fountain of Youth. Or they are looking for different opportunities or a different way of life. I fall into that category, a fresh start, a completely different way of life. You sever all past relationshps—in a church or whatever—and make a brand new start. Life down here is entirely different, a different feeling, a different structure, extremely casual. I would call it, 'So What?.'"[14]

The 1972 survey I have referred to found the same problem. The percentage of those whose activity recently had tapered off involved about a third of all church members. Out of sixteen possible reasons, lack of time was viewed as the major culprit. Time is scarce and there are too many social and cultural rivals for the church's time. In the competition, the church comes in second.[15]

For our evangelism to touch the lives of these people, we must be sensitive to Calvin's opening words in the *Institutes of the Christian Religion*. Under the heading, "Without knowledge of self there is no knowledge of God," Calvin

Evangelism: Doing Justice and Preaching Grace

begins: "Nearly all the wisdom we possess, that is to say, true and sound wisdom, consists of two parts: the knowledge of God and of ourselves. But, while joined by many bonds, which one precedes and brings forth the other is not easy to discern."[16] Calvin's "order of right teaching" begins with the knowledge of God, but even then, he is never far away from the knowledge of man. Salvation, if we may paraphrase loosely, is humanization, and humanization is salvation.

Seen in this perspective, evangelism is the announcement of the restoration of humanity, of fallen imagehood redeemed in Christ "the image of God" (Eph. 4:24; Col. 3:10). Humanity has been imprisoned by man's spiritual and moral irresponsibility. Our full calling to personhood, to regal service in our covenant humanity (Gen. 1:26–28), has been enslaved to sin. Evangelism announces the liberating work of God as in Christ He fashions a new humanity (2 Cor. 5:17). At Calvary Jesus Christ begins the rebuilding of our humanity. And no one, and no organization, may threaten the new liberty we possess as children of God. The church is not our new oppressor but the place where we find our fulfillment as the new humanity (Eph. 1:21–22).

Evangelism as a Call to Celebration

The happy hedonists find the fulfillment of life's purpose in momentary pleasures or a succession of pleasure-satisfying activities. They are happy because they exude complete satisfaction with what they are doing. They are hedonists in their idolization of leisure pursuits. Their complaints about the church were expressed to Hale with comments like these: "The church doesn't want me to have a good time," and "Compared to other excitements I can find or buy, the church can't compete." A burned-out minister reflects his frustration over the happy hedonist: "They come down here for leisure. What can you do?" A retiree from Michigan puts it his way: "You've got so many choices here that my church is no longer the most important thing." Life is too short for the solemnity of the church.

If Jesus Is the Answer, What Are the Questions?

To meet these needs, evangelism must display again the joy of total sacrifice for the treasure of the kingdom. Evangelism flows out of the celebration of the good pleasure of the Father—joy in heaven over the sinner who repents (Luke 15:7). It does not celebrate ecclesiastical authority in matters of demon possession but joy in matters of heavenly obsession (Luke 10:20). "Life is too deep" for the solemnity of the church. Evangelism turned a Philippian prison cell into a play pen of the Spirit, with songs at midnight (Acts 16:25). In Christ the hurried, last-minute meal of the Passover before liberation became the Lord's Supper, the wedding feast of the Lamb before the marriage's final consummation (Luke 22:16, 18). It makes worship good, clean fun and thorns-in-the-flesh celebrations of God's sufficient grace (2 Cor. 12:7–9).

Evangelism as a Call to Justice

The largest group of the unchurched Hale calls the publicans. They see discrepancies in the church's life, a dissonance that has made them get up and leave the room. They charge that church people are hypocrites, phonies, fakers. A chemical plant worker in Maine told Hale, "As far as I am concerned, the [church people] are no different from anybody else." A farmer in Polk County, Nebraska, is angry: "Every church I have gone to any length of time at all I have run into the same phony people." Hale's list is a long one: "an old Huey Long politician—crooked as can be; a millionaire on a country-town law-practice income—who is the pillar of the church"; a preacher, "one of the biggest crooks I ever ran into in my life. In church, he was Goody Two-Shoes, but outside he was a cheat in business dealings."

Where do we go to hear the voices of the publicans? To the black ghettos of the inner city, to the Hispanics picking our tomatoes in the fields, to the children who watch our family arguments at the dinner table, to the silent Asian embittered by our Fu-Manchu caricatures of the East.

How shall we touch them? Evangelism must become gospel show-and-tell, showing mercy and preaching grace.

Evangelism: Doing Justice and Preaching Grace

Jesus heralded the coming of the kingdom before the paralytic with two words: "Rise up and walk" and "Your sins are forgiven." Our church bells ring only one of those notes. Orlando Costas, a Hispanic missiologist, puts it this way: "As members of the eschatological community of salvation, Christians are called to interpret Christ's saving work by actualizing in their everyday life the essential characteristics of salvation. Having been born into the family of God, they must actualize God's love in the fellowship of faith and in their relations with the rest of the world. Their experience of liberation from the power of sin and death requires of them the manifestation of God's *shalom* in their life (i.e., a life of reconciliation, freedom, and fullness). Their participation in the life of God's kingdom demands of them a commitment to justice."[17]

The evangelists of the first century were not simply trying to imitate Jesus. Rather, Jesus Christ was living in them. "Instead of one Jesus Christ walking around Jerusalem there were now—and I say it reverently—one hundred and twenty Jesus Christs there. As Martin Luther described it, they were 'Little Christs,' men in whom Jesus Christ was continuing to live His life. They had undergone a fantastic spiritual transformation that revolutionized every aspect of their lives—the moral, the social, the economic. Jesus Christ touched them with His power and they, in turn, touched their world with power. They became revolutionaries, Christian style. They touched hypocrisy and turned it into reality. They touched immorality and turned it into purity. They touched slavery and turned it into liberty. They touched cruelty and turned it into charity. They touched snobbery and turned it into equality."[18]

Evangelism in Terms of What the Church Gives

It's time now to flip our coin. We have been defining evangelism in terms of what some call felt needs. Now let's look again in terms of felt givens, the Bible's own lexicon of categories.

Many of us will probably do that very comfortably with

the formulations of the written creeds that make up our church's confession of faith. We can remind ourselves of those ecclesiastical ancestors who saw the conversion of pagans and the planting of the church as important aspects of the mission of the church. Backward in time we go to the Reformation creeds and beyond. Wasn't the preaching of the Word one of the marks of the sixteenth-century church?

Allow me to unsettle you a bit. In his book *The Dispersion of the People of God* Richard De Ridder carries on a lover's quarrel with such standards. He examines specifically one set of continental creeds and asks, "Where is missions? Where is evangelism?" He asks it much more nicely than I do. But there is more than a tinge of skepticism in both his voice and mine. Still circling within the orbit of a Corpus Christianum mentality, the church of the Reformation creeds is a static, rather quiet corner in the world. It is busy, to be sure, with its own housecleaning, but it has little concept of inviting in the neighbors to gossip the gospel. "The church becomes only the place where certain things are done . . . and is not looked upon as a group which God has called into existence to do something. The marks of the church need to be placed decisively within the framework of the church's mission. This is where they were first set. For in Acts 2:42 the teaching, fellowship, breaking of bread, and prayers of the newly-formed Spirit-filled and Spirit-enlarged disciple fellowship is described within the missionary context of the Pentecost story from which it cannot be extracted."[19]

Evangelism is not a narrowed concern of those who "like that sort of thing." It is a call to confess the saving lordship of Christ. It cannot be narrowed to become maximum attention to a minimum "gospel core," a gospel packaging that isolates "discipling" from "perfecting," Jesus as Savior from Jesus as Lord. It is a call to take our jargon words and retool. Terms like *kerygma* (proclamation), *diakonia,* (service), *koinonia* (fellowship), and *leiturgia* (worship), are not isolated bits and pieces of the kingdom, living by themselves in rooms with closed doors. They are different ways of describing the same room. One door into that room we call kerygma, another diakonia, still another koinonia.

Kerygma, the proclamation of the kingdom, revolves around the idea of announcement by the king's herald, whether a John the Baptist (Matt. 3:2) or a Paul (Acts 28:31). But the kerygma center of attention is never the herald. It is the King he heralds. A famous London preacher was recently asked to conduct a mission at Cambridge University. "I hear you are going to lecture to the students at Cambridge," remarked a friend. "No," he replied. "I am going to talk to a group of sinners about Jesus Christ."[20] Like the Lord's Supper, our announcement of the kingdom in Christ is still a combined word-and-deed ministry. We extend the cup in the name of Jesus. *Kerygma* is the biblical word that focuses on the name.

During the Tell-Scotland campaign in the mid 1950s, a minister in the north wrote to the organizers at the movement's headquarters in Glasgow: "We have our committees organized, our literature prepared, our schedules set, our promotion underway. We are ready now to take part in 'Tell-Scotland.' But, pray, tell me, what are we to tell Scotland?"

How strong is the danger of our becoming runners from Marathon who come stumbling into the presence of the king after our long run and gasp out in our triumph of endurance, "I've forgotten the message"? How unfounded is this fear that seems to dominate much of the writing and theorizing of people like Donald McGavran? I have met more than one medical missionary on the "foreign" field who has full commitment to the doctrines of sovereign grace and is a genius with a scalpel, but is a shy kindergartner when it comes to sharing his faith. I have known professors of theology who are experts in the gospel message but have never shared it over a cup of coffee with a distraught neighbor whose children are on drugs.

Evangelism is also what Jesus Christ does through the church's *koinonia*, her fellowship. The newness of the kingdom is proclaimed through koinonia. It is the setting in which the contagion of the Christian hope is communicated. But it is even more than that. The great Methodist evangelist Donald Soper exclaims, "If it is from Kerygma that the Christian faith is taught, it is within Koinonia that the Christian faith is caught."[21] Every summer, Dr. Jack Miller at Westminster Theological Seminary takes a large group of students and church members with him for three weeks of street preaching in Dublin, Ireland. They are on the streets almost all day long, witnessing, sharing (koinonia-ing) the gospel. Everyone they speak with is invited to a common meal held in the evening at a nearby church. The meal is quite simple. There are singing, some testimonies, and prayer. Here the unchurched, the curious, the converts, are given a taste of koinonia. One student said to me after that trip, "I think the most effective part of our ministry is carried on at the meal table. The guests see the church suddenly as a caring, sharing fellowship; their bargain with God is sealed by a cup of coffee."

Many of us, along with our churches, are getting fat with meals we still label "fellowship." But we are not growing. The difference is in whom we invite to the table.

For this who feel exploited and manipulated, the Bible reminds us of a third category, *Diakonia* is the service of a slave of the new kingdom. Jesus evangelized on earth through His service (Luke 19:10). The unfolding of His gospel ministry was under the compulsion of the servant's "I must" (Matt. 16:21; Luke 24:26). He who served as one in the midst of us (Luke 22:27) has given us an example. Are we, as His servants, greater than our Master (John 13:15)?

Are our diaconal programs oriented to evangelism? Philip, set apart to wait on tables in Acts 6, "proclaims Christ" in Samaria as an evangelist (Acts 8:5–7). And the gospel door opens racially for the first time in New Testament history. Paul's advice is to "do good to all men, and especially to those who are of the household of faith" (Gal. 6:10). In the process of translating that into reality, it comes out, "Do good to all men if you have the money and the time, but remember our budget is small and the church has an awful lot of needs right at home. Concentrate, you deacons, on the saints."

Evangelism: Doing Justice and Preaching Grace

Should the church get involved in questions of social justice? Was it not a question of equity over food distribution that required the apostles to appoint the seven (Acts 6:1–3)? Should not the office of deacon be the place where the world sees real compassion for the "sinned against," the racially brutalized? Isn't love simply the command of God to be just in our actions? Bill Milliken calls it "tough love." On the street corners of the world's inner cities the evangelical too often has been standing, singing, "Take the world and give me Jesus." And now we have what we asked for. We have Jesus and the world has been taken away from us.

What is the first priority of inner-city evangelism? Leighton Ford heard this answer: "The people in the inner city have heard so many raps they are disenchanted. We have to love people without strings attached and give our message off the springboard of involvement. This is the rap that will be heard."[22] Notice that the gospel words are not minimized. The idea is that service must maximize them.

There is also *leiturgia* as evangelism, worship as the proclamation of the kingdom to the unchurched.

Worship becomes a herald of the king's coming. The coming of the wise men to the Christ child is a coming to worship. And in it is foreshadowed the ingathering of the nations. Setting forth God's praise, declaring His excellence, is supremely an act of worship, but it is worship that witnesses before the nations to the true and living God. (Ps. 107:21, 22). Isaiah pictures the nations being drawn to God's feast in Mount Zion. It is a meeting for worship (Isa. 2:2–4; 56:6–8).

The New Testament does not substantially change that focus. It merely directs it to Christ. The Mount of God is indeed exalted. It is exalted to where Christ is, seated at the right hand of the Father (1 Peter 2:9–11). Evangelism summons the world to the city with foundations, whose Builder and Maker is God. So Paul can think of his ministry as the assembling of a chorus of praise from the lips of the Gentiles (Rom. 15:6, 9–11). The fruit of his evangelism is an act of worship, "the offering of the Gentiles" (Rom. 15:16).

If Jesus Is the Answer, What Are the Questions?

How much of our worship shows forth the celebration of evangelism? How much of our evangelism smells of sawdust and not the stars of heaven? What must be done to keep the church from sleeping through the revolution of the gospel by trivializing and boring it to hell? (I am using the term *hell* in its theological sense.) Why must the happy hedonists go to football games to do their shouting, to the movies to do their crying, and to church to do their freezing?

I've said enough. Probably too much. I remind you of the words of a great pioneer missionary of the Reformed Church in America, Dr. John Van Ess of Persia. After several days of a missionary conference and much talk and planning, he rose. "Brethren," he said, "I am sure this talk of strategy is always very good. But really we have only one strategy: telling people about Jesus!"

3

Evangelism and Justice: Setting Things Right

The quest for the meaning of evangelism is studded with Greek words—*kerygma, koinonia, leiturgia,* and *diakonia* (proclamation, fellowship, worship and service). There is a fifth, *dikaiōma,* which I have saved for this chapter. It is probably the most controversial. It is easily the most misunderstood. But it is certainly the most important in dealing with the largest category of the unchurched.

That category is what Hale calls the publicans. In one respect, we will be covering more than just the publicans. The publicans are omnipresent among the unchurched. Their complaints about the church are repeated in all the other categories. They see the Christian as leading two lives, "Inside," says one of the informants, "the church member thinks he is Jesus Christ himself, he is so good. Outside, you can't tell him from anybody else." An army colonel in Maine puts it succinctly: "Church services in organized Christianity represent nothing more than a sacred canopy which covers the previous week's debauchery of its members."[1]

The poor reflect their anger. "If you ain't got the money, you ain't in." A Danish war bride, married to a Mexican-American, tastes prejudice in a California church. "Certain remarks were made by certain people," she said. "We won't go to that church again." A man in a youth commune in Maine views the church members as Pharisees. "It doesn't do any good to see Richard Nixon and Gerald Ford go to church. When they come out, they—oh, it's just like they don't believe anymore. If a person goes to church, he should live up to it."[2]

All of these outcries are demands for justice, for faithfulness to our confession. Their instincts tell them something is wrong with a gospel sold at the front door like the *Saturday Evening Post* thirty years ago, but blind to the slum in the back yard. They may not know what the gospel is. But they know what's right, what's fair. They are tired of gospel used-car salesmen who sell vehicles with three pistons missing.

If evangelism is to meet all the needs of the publicans, the church will have to recruit an army of good Samaritans. And reality that will touch their felt needs is expressed in the Greek word *Dikaiōma*, the righteous deed, the doing of justice. Sidney Rooy calls it "Love in action."[3] Love (*ahab*), according to the Old Testament, is more than affection or a Hollywood-style emotion. It is conduct characteristic of affection. Within the ancient Near-Eastern traditions of religion, "love" was a characteristic term used in political life. It was the bond between the king and his subjects. It meant loyalty, fidelity, obedience.[4] It also meant justice. To love one's neighbor was to do justice to the neighbor. So love could be commanded. Israel was to love the resident alien by giving the alien food and clothing (Deut. 10:18–19).

By displaying this justice, Israel witnessed to the nations. How will all the nations be blessed in Abraham? Genesis 18:19 responds, "I have chosen him, so that he will direct his children and his household after him to keep the way of the LORD by doing what is right and just, *so that* the LORD will bring about for Abraham what he has promised him." How did Saul dishonor the Lord before the Philistines? By not doing justly (1 Sam. 13). Solomon asked for wisdom to deal justly with the resident alien "so that all the peoples of the earth may know your Name" (1 Kings 8:43). The queen of Sheba marveled at the wisdom of Solomon's justice (1 Kings 10:4, 6–7). And the nations marveled with her (1 Kings 10:23–24). The apostasy of Israel that closes the pages of the Old Testament is measured in terms of urban injustice (Amos 5:12; 6:12; 8:5). And the nations who witnessed this injustice were called on to perform the other task of the Old Testament witness; they became the executioners of God's wrath, casting the first stone in judgment.

The New Testament church does not escape the obligations of doing justly for evangelism. We are marked as those who hunger and thirst after righteousness (Matt. 5:6). And that righteousness, as Herman Ridderbos points out, is not righteousness in the Pauline sense of imputed forensic righteousness. It is the kingly justice that God has promised for the salvation of the oppressed and the outcasts. It is the kingly justice that God has promised the Messiah would bring.[5] We live in a new day, the day of the promised King. And His coming was to be a coming on behalf of justice for all, "fairness for the afflicted of the earth" (see Isa. 11:1–5). The Old Testament promise of the Messiah's jubilee year meant justice and freedom for the oppressed, the broken (Isa. 61:1–2). In Christ the jubilee year of restoration for society has begun (Luke 4:17–21).

So James calls us to a faith that works. And it works in terms of the poor and the hungry (James 2:14–17). He startles us by underlining the nature of faith as the exercise of hope in justice. "You see that a person is justified by what he does and not by faith alone" (James 2:24). The doing of justice becomes the distinguishing mark of the people of God before the world. "This is how we know who the children of God are and who the children of the devil are: Anyone who does not do what is just is not a child of God; neither is anyone who does not love his brother" (1 John 3:10). For John, love and justice intermingle. In love and justice we find the lived-out reality of knowing God (1 John 2:29; 4:7–8).

How can the church model out this *dikaiōma* part of evangelism? In doing it, it faces at least two great dangers.

Evangelism: Doing Justice and Preaching Grace

On the one hand, it can remake evangelism into just one more Christian word for political involvement or social action. The social-gospel history reminds us that that danger is always real. Evangelism can become a loose term for freedom marches, the boycotting of South African investments, and antinuclear demonstrations. On the other hand, the call for justice as an intrinsic part of evangelism can be reduced to protesting pornographic films, contributing to special offerings for the "boat people," and being a decent and pleasant person at the office or school.

Hindrances to Dikaiōma Evangelism Among the Publicans

First, I want to warn against at least a couple of ways in which we can inhibit this part of evangelism in our methods.

Sympathy, Not Compassion

How is sympathy a hindrance to evangelism? Aren't we all called to identify with the sinner in his need? Yes, but the question is how. Depending on that how, sympathy is not necessarily biblical compassion.

Over seven years of my twelve in Korea as a foreign missionary were spent doing evangelistic work with prostitutes. My initiation into that ministry came simply because of the large number of those "unreached peoples" and because I thought that they were rather clearly sinners. I saw them as in rebellion against God and needing repentance. And I went calling them to faith. I defined their needs in terms of how I had seen needs in a North American pastorate.

The fruits of my initial encounters were very few. The young women listened but never left prostitution. No one changed. The breakthrough came when one person began to change: I changed. As I worked with the women, I gathered more information about the system of which they were a part. I learned that many of them had entered prostitution because it was often the only work they could find in an Asian, male-dominated, culture. The war had destroyed their links with the extended family system. And often they were the senior breadwinners. There were brothers and sisters to take care of. Frequently the young women came from rural homes, looking for quick money in the big city. Personal problems at home or a bad economic year sent them looking for a better way. They were met at the trains by the pimps, who offered them a place to stay for the night. In the home they were gang-raped. When they got ready to leave, they were informed they had to pay for room and board. They couldn't and found prostitution the only way to pay their debts. After a few weeks of this, their debt was paid for by another brothel owner, and they were moved closer to the 38th parallel. They had become slaves of a system from which they could never break free. Their debts were always higher than their ability to pay. They found themselves imprisoned and oppressed, their humanity buried in shame and guilt.

All this information began to change my attitude. I started suspecting my own early motivations. Was it sin I had really seen? Or the violation of middle-class morality? At this stage, my early sympathies seemed more like cultural morality. I became compassionate. What is the difference?

I discovered that a person is not only a sinner. He or she is also sinned against. My cultural background in white, North American churches had oriented me almost exclusively to seeing a person as the subject of sin. But not the object of sin. Seeking the various factors that kept women in prostitution opened my eyes to that new dimension.

Compassion is more than maternal tenderness, more than Pharaoh's daughter seeing the baby Moses crying. It is Pharaoh's daughter seeing the baby of an oppressed Hebrew crying (Exod. 2:6). It is tenderness translated into action on behalf of the sinned against. "I have indeed seen the misery of my people," the Lord said to Moses at the burning bush. "I have heard them crying out . . . I am concerned about their suffering. So I have come down to rescue them" (Exod. 3:7–8).

Evangelism: Doing Justice and Preaching Grace

The compassion of our Lord reached out to feed over four thousand. And the multitude that compelled Him to action included "the lame, the blind, the crippled, the dumb and many others" (Matt. 15:30). Two blind men on the way to Jericho (Matt. 20:34) and a widow with an only son taken in death (Luke 7:12–13) also touched the springs of His concern. These categories of people are important in understanding His messianic compassion. They are those who have been excluded from the kingdom by the pettiness of the Pharisees. They are those who live in a world without the sheltering concern of the kinsman, widows whose houses are devoured by the Pharisee (Matt. 23:14), and the handicapped whose lifestyle has forced them to the edge of an unfeeling society. Through Jesus' kingdom compassion they begin to taste the power of the new day that has come, the restoration of society that God their only Kinsman has begun to give. From the lower brackets of society, they are lifted up by Jesus' regal power to the edge of the kingdom and God's new just order for the Creation.

What does all of this have to do with evangelizing the publicans? A gospel that does not address people as the sinned-against poses a lot of problems for the publican, the sinned-against. Either he rejects the gospel or sees it as an opiate.

This point is well illustrated by Raymond Fung, an industrial evangelist in Hong Kong. As a result of helping to resolve a labor dispute, he came to know a textile worker in his early forties. The worker would occasionally come to Fung's office for a chat when he could spare the time. At Fung's urging, he came to church one Sunday at the cost of a day's wages. After the service they went to lunch. The worker said, "Well, the sermon hit me. You know, what the preacher said is true of me—laziness, a violent temper, and addiction to cheap entertainment. I guess he was talking about me all right." Fung held his breath, trying to keep down his excitement. "But," the man continued, "there is nothing there about my boss—employing child laborers, not giving us legally required holidays, putting on false labels, and forcing us to do overtime. . . ." Fung's heart sank. He was sad, he said, "not simply because this friend of mine is most unlikely to go to church again, but more because there are quite a number of factory owners in the congregation who should benefit from the textile worker's observation."[6]

The textile worker was a publican. He had tasted the impact of the gospel. But he had tasted also its one-sided presentation—an evangelistic message that did not speak to the needs of those who have been sinned against. The gospel that ignores the sinned-against may work among the middle class, but it cannot possibly work among the overwhelming majority in Asia or the United States—publican peasants and workers. It conveys too much superiority, condescension, yes even pity, to be credible. What is missing is compassion. Compassion becomes possible when we perceive people as the sinned-against, as well as the sinning.

At the heart of compassion is the idea of "suffering with" (Rom. 8:17), involvement in the pain of the publican's sense of what is "not right."[7] It invites the publican inside. It does not keep him outside looking in. It invites people to look at Jesus and address Him as "You" rather than "Him."

At one time I had an experience in Korea almost exactly like that of Fung in Hong Kong. I was present when an evangelist was invited by the factory owner to preach over a loudspeaker to the shop-floor workers. It was plain that no one was listening to him. The workers thought he was talking nonsense. Next day the loudspeaker wire was cut. A week or so later, in a small group of those factory workers meeting at lunch for a fifteen-minute Bible study, I used the same text the evangelist had used. One or two of the men had visited my home and we had shared a meal together. There was a positive response.

Talk, Not Truth

Publicans are tired of talk. They suffer from "information overload." Their "limited intake capacity" has been limited even more by what they have seen in the church, not by what they have heard. One of the most famous publicans is Karl Marx. In London's Highgate Cemetery a huge granite

Evangelism: Doing Justice and Preaching Grace

pillar stands on top of his grave. Chiseled on the granite is the motto of many publicans: "The philosophers have only interpreted the world in various ways; the point however is to change it!" Talk is not cheap for the publican. But it is cheapened for him by the evangelist whose only concept of truth is propositional verbalization.

Let me say right now that I am not trying to shift away from a confidence in truth as the given word of the God who speaks. Truth had a verbal nature for Paul. He could tell it (Rom. 9:1; 2 Cor. 12:6). It was a sacred deposit every evangelist had to guard as a steward (1 Cor. 15:3; 2 Thess. 2:15).

What we need to stress is seeing truth as not simply an objective word verified propositionally by God. The heart of truth is God in covenant faithfulness to Himself. Truth is the acting out by word and deed of God's faithfulness to Himself and to people. It is the constancy of God in covenant with His creation.[8] "They will be my people, and I will be faithful and righteous to them as their God" (Zech. 8:8).

And, as the mirrors of God, we are called to "do truth" (1 John 1:6). We are to be children of the light. And the fruit of that light consists in all goodness and justice and truth (Eph. 5:9). We are to stand firm, wearing the breastplate of righteousness or justice (Eph. 6:14). What is the opposite of truth in Scripture? Most of us would quickly answer error. But the most common answer is disobedience, infidelity, forsaking the covenant.

How does one identify the "sound doctrine" that Paul so frequently commends? Does one begin making theological heresy lists, boxes of 3x5 cards filled with doctrinal mistakes? No, one focuses on the context of living, acting or doing the truth among the covenant people of God. In the pastoral epistles where the term *sound doctrine* occurs, the focus is repeatedly on a life lived in faithfulness to God and to others. What is "contrary to the sound doctrine" (1 Tim. 1:10)? It is the attitude and actions of "lawbreakers and rebels, the ungodly and sinful, the unholy and irreligious . . . those who kill their fathers or mothers . . . mur-

Evangelism and Justice: Setting Things Right

derers . . . adulterers and perverts . . . slave traders and liars and perjurers" (1 Tim. 1:9–10; cf. 1 Tim. 4:6ff.; 2 Tim. 4:1ff.; Titus 1:9ff.; 2:1ff.). The teachers of "sound doctrine" are the spiritually mature. Their teaching will be not merely in the words they utter but in the lives they use to demonstrate the just rule of God. So "teaching" must be entrusted to "reliable men who will also be qualified to teach others" (2 Tim. 2:2; cf. 1 Tim. 6:3–5).

We can talk about evangelism in words and propositions. But the test of whether "teachings" and "doctrines" are "sound" must always be their function of covenant faithfulness. Testing the spirits (1 John 4:1) is done in discerning love in each other and working justice for each other. So in John's letter, testing the spirits and loving one another are always seen together. John is not commanding us to be suspicious of other people and their intellectual formulas when he calls us to "test the spirits." It is a command to embrace, respond justly, and be bound to each other. Why? Because God embraces, responds justly, and is bound to us.

The publicans in our church neighborhoods are not waiting for talk but for truth. They are waiting for the good news God speaks in Isaiah 58. "Is not this the kind of fasting I have chosen: to loose the chains of injustice and untie the cords of the yoke, to set the oppressed free and break every yoke? Is it not to share your food with the hungry and to provide the poor wanderer with shelter . . . ? Then your light will break forth like the dawn, and . . . your righteousness will go before you" (Isa. 58:6–8).

In the Fourth Ward Clinic of Houston, Texas is an example of biblical truth. In a black ghetto of that city, seven thousand poor people are packed into huge blocks of flats. There Dr. Bob Eckert started a medical clinic in 1968. Dr. Eckert knew that door-to-door evangelism in that ghetto would elicit only one human response: "Poor talkative little Christianity." He set up a medical clinic that offered free treatment. It began with a table, a chair, three workers, and four patients on the first day. Now one hundred to two hundred are served every day. Dr. Eckert's goal

49

Evangelism: Doing Justice and Preaching Grace

has not changed. "We're not here to doctor. We are here to share the Lord Jesus. The medical practice is something that comes out of the love God has for people." Often people ask to be prayed for. They sense there is truth in that place.[9]

The publicans ask us for truth. They will find it in a commitment to the simple lifestyle on the part of the church. They will hear it when they hear God's people asking, "Where is the threshhold of my pain in sacrifice as a citizen of the kingdom? What shall I leave so that the publican may find? Where must I go so that they may come?"

Models of Dikaiōma Evangelism Among the Publicans

In summary of what I have said so far, the really effective kind of evangelism is what may be called holistic evangelism. Perhaps a more comfortable title for it would be lordship evangelism. We are recognizing that evangelism can never be seen "in isolation from the critical questions and events that shape the context in which the gospel must be lived and proclaimed. The scope of our evangelism must be at least as pervasive as the power of sin itself."[10] And at the heart of whatever we do is our acknowledgment of the kingdom reign of Christ over all of life. In the tension between the already and the not yet of the kingdom, evangelism announces the place where our victory celebration has already begun—Calvary. And it holds up the place where our victory practice leads us—the new Jerusalem. And in between, it looks for models where we may see the concerns of the publican treated with integrity—models that do not manipulate situations into opportunistic occasions for springboard evangelism, models that do not make service and justice into some sort of pre-evangelism (warranted in its own right) occasions for tongue-tied evangelism. I am talking about personal and public discipleship.

The third world will furnish most of the experiments. What is traditionally called "foreign missions" has always

50

had more freedom to experiment in this area than the church here. Now it's time to learn from the world body of Christ.

Our theological seminaries and mass-evangelism interests can learn much from the Latin American Institute of In-Depth Evangelism. INDEPTH emerged out of the earlier and well-publicized "Evangelism in Depth" movement. The core of its program is captured in the formula R^2AC: "Renovation, renewal, action and consolidation." Team members are located in Brazil, Costa Rica, and the Caribbean coast of Central America. This movement seeks to assist groups of believers, churches, denominations, and regional fellowships through a process of reflection on Scripture, themselves, and their situation. In Brazil, where most of its field work is focused, it is moving away from the large regional or national movement that characterized the older "Evangelism in Depth" movements of the 1960s. These former campaigns, it argues, did too little to effect permanent change in the churches' evangelistic lifestyle. They related too superficially to the realities and needs of the churches and their contexts. The new movement calls for four-dimensional growth through an emphasis on (1) theological understanding, (2) relatedness to socio-economic and cultural context, (3) numerical growth, and (4) organizational growth. Much of its philosophy of approach can be seen in the writings of one of its chief formulators, Orlando Costas.[11]

This holistic approach is also reflected in the work of the Elizabeth Native Interior Mission of Liberia. Founded some twenty years ago by an independent black American missionary known as Mother George, the Mission is now under the direction of Augustus B. Marwieh, a Liberian. In the middle and late 1960s, an evangelistic campaign by Marwieh and others discovered interior populations highly receptive to the gospel. But the traditional Western system of the Mission-station approach was too inflexible to reach them. Marwieh began to transform this approach into a vocational, agricultural, and community-based approach. Beginning in 1972, he established a system of community farms and organized village store cooperatives. With Mar-wieh's active encouragement, worship in the interior churches became alive with thoroughly indigenous choral music—African celebrations of Christ. In addition, lay evangelist missionaries are carrying the gospel further in-land and across the border into the Ivory Coast. National concern for development is married to the spiritual dimen-sions of development. [12]

In the United States, one of the most exciting models on a congregational level is that of the Voice of Calvary in Mendenhall, Mississippi. Founded by John Perkins, the program had its beginnings in Perkins' childhood experi-ences in Mississippi. When at the age of sixteen, his older brother was killed by a white marshal, Perkins left Mississippi, vowing never to return. In 1957 Perkins be-came a Christian and later returned to his home state. He and his wife organized rural home Bible studies and held tent meetings that included literacy programs. In 1960 he founded the Voice of Calvary Bible Institute. And this became the center not only for Bible study but for a tutoring and lunch program for elementary children and a leadership training program for teenagers. By the end of the decade, Perkins had helped organize some thirty agricultural and economic cooperatives in the state.

During the 1969 Christmas holidays, the vision of Per-kins took another shape. A boycott of the Mendenhall shopping district indirectly led to the jailing and severe beating of Perkins and some of his colleagues. During a time of prolonged hospitalization, Perkins came to see that there was no hope in the power of violence but only in the love of Christ. The VOC community had to "come together, to become God's people, His church, for anything good to happen in Mendenhall."

With legal help from Sargeant Shriver's law firm, a foun-dation was formed to serve as a channel for the small but growing support from white Christian friends. In 1971 a college scholarship fund was established; in 1972, a Chris-tian Youth and Vocational Center; and a health center in 1973. In 1974 there came into being in Jackson,

Evangelism and Justice: Setting Things Right

Mississippi, People Development, Inc., an agency for funding housing renewal and other black business enterprises. Out of all this has come an integrating movement. Campus evangelism, tutoring programs, vocational- and building-trades training, family and business counseling, and Bible study are merged into a holistic model.

"How do we get rid of the welfare system in America?" Perkins asked recently. "I am convinced that this issue, which is basically how we relate our resources and Christian faith to the needs of human beings around us, is the crisis by which Jesus will judge us and our country. If we face this question head on, we will have no alternative but to become the church."

Within the Reformed community is the model being built now by a congregation of the Presbyterian Church in America in St. Louis, Missouri. The Grace and Peace Fellowship began in 1969 in a neighborhood then 65 percent black, with a high level of petty crime. A two-story semicommercial building was purchased in the center of the neighborhood. At present 200 people meet for worship, with the membership either of quite a low income or well off. Black population in the area remains transient. In 1977 the group decided to keep membership at the level of 150 to 250 people. In 1978 two other congregations were started in different neighborhoods, one nearly middle class, the other in an old neighborhood that is now beginning to be redeveloped.

Over the years, the church has been the center around which a large number of lordship ministries have begun. In 1975 they began what has come to be called the "Neighborhood Service." It is a program of home visitation by a full-time female deacon fully employed by the church, remedial-reading programs carried on by members, counseling offered to teenagers and to families. A food cooperative was formed, supplemented by food service to welfare-referred individuals. There is a prison ministry and a home for street people who need temporary housing. Financially the most ambitious program is the Cornerstone Foundation, now a not-for-profit housing corporation of twelve

Evangelism: Doing Justice and Preaching Grace

units. The Foundation purchases abandoned housing units, rebulds them with volunteer labor, and offers them for rent at low cost to the poor who face eviction in the wake of urban renewal. One Christian family from the church is seeded into the renovated building and commits itself to an evangelistic and serving ministry among the tenants. In the planning stages now is an urban coalition with other city churches to establish a Christian school, not only for the church's children but also for children of the neighborhoods. Members are encouraged to move into the neighborhood where the church centers its ministry and exercise their gifts for service-evangelism.

There are models of *dikaiōma* evangelism on a personal level. Take Bill Iversen, for example. He bought a lunch counter across from an inner-city high school in his search for publicans. When Newark was devastated by race riots some years back, Bill's lunch stand was one of the few buildings untouched by the rioters. He was saying something that people were hearing. He also sponsors inner-city block parties. A street is blocked off, people sing and eat together. Young people give dramatic presentations of the gospel. In one presentation a man is chained to a wall and several keys are handed up to him one at a time. One is labeled "green power," another "black power," and there are others with other labels, but none of them can open the lock. Finally a key is handed up called "love power," and the man is freed. He then turns to the crowd and tells them how the love of Jesus has set him free.

But where do the Bill Iversens start? How do you begin with publicans? First, find them. They are everywhere— the lonely widow on your block who lost her husband four months ago, the Moonie selling flowers at the airport, the blue-collar worker whose life revolves around the lathe in his basement. Befriend them; have a cup of coffee with the widow, take a minute to talk with the Moonie, make a visit to that basement workshop of the lathe operator. Then what? "How do you begin an evangelistic conversation?" may be what you want to ask now.

It may start with a lot of listening. Rein in your impa-

Evangelism and Justice: Setting Things Right

tience after that Sunday morning message on witnessing. Find out where they are coming from. What has made them publicans?

Over a cup of coffee, the widow confesses, "Sometimes I get so lonely I could climb these walls." First, tell her there is a God who loves her so intimately that the very hairs on her head are numbered. This God is personal and she can pray to Him. He is present and struggling with her, and desires a covenant-fellowship with her."[13] The words are bare ones. Adorn them with a genuine compassion that the publican can taste and feel. Fred Allen used to say that "you could take all of the sincerity in Hollywood and stuff it in a gnat's navel and leave enough room for two caraway seeds and an agent's heart!" There are many publicans who could say that of Christians. Show them otherwise.

George Hunter, Secretary for Evangelism of the United Methodist Church, writes of his meeting a pretty devotee of the Hare Krishna cult in Chicago's O'Hare airport. She began the conversation by saying, "Excuse me, sir, but all of the handsome gentlemen are wearing carnations today. May I give you one?" Hunter continues, "She got my attention. We briefly conversed, and I remember saying: 'Look, I know you're into this now—but it will leave you hollow and let-down later. Whenever that happens, telephone me collect any time, day or night.' I gave her my card. She looked aside to be sure her partners were busy elsewhere; her eyes teared, and her voice trembled as she almost whispered—'Thank you, Mr. Hunter, I just might do that.'"[14]

Bob DeMoss, the Director of Partnership in Mission, a service agency for world missions, read Raymond Fung's essay referred to earlier. The day before he read it, he was sharing the gospel with a stranger in a local park. The person saw little relevance of the gospel to her. But she admitted that in her ten years as a woman manager in industry she experienced much injustice and felt sinned against. At the time Bob spoke to her, he was unable to use her own recognition of "being sinned against" as part of his sharing the gospel.

Evangelism: Doing Justice and Preaching Grace

Fung's article changed that. Some time later he was at the beach very early in the morning playing his guitar. Two young brothers, aged ten and fifteen, sat down to listen. They talked about "being on their own since our parents don't live with us any longer." As they talked, Bob's compassion took control and he spoke openly of their being sinned against. From that felt need, he spoke of the God who can "deliver us from evil" if we submit to his lordship.

What about an evangelistic survey for our neighborhoods that begins by asking, "What do you believe the church should be doing in this community to help people?" Ask your shopkeepers, your teachers, your unskilled laborers. Ask them if they feel the church has helped in the past. "What causes or services have you been involved in that you believe were very significant—causes that Christ would have been involved in if He had been here?" "Have you ever considered giving your whole life to the purposes of Christ for people?" Take their suggestions to the elders and deacons, share them with your congregation. Settle on several as priorities for that community of faith. Go back to the people who made these suggestions and share your conclusions. Invite them to join you in this expression of ministry.

Let people know that by giving their allegiance to Christ they will be embarking on a great campaign to banish war and poverty and injustice, to set up a life where love and service and justice have taken the place of selfishness and power. Let people know that the church that sends out this manifesto plans to be an advance copy of the new world order it preaches. Donald Soper, a British Methodist bishop, writes, "The credentials of an evangelist are his experience of God as a Father and his vision and programme for a new world; if these are his, he must become a missionary."[15] Perhaps our biggest problem is the minimization of the gospel's outer limits to an evangelistic core. Our evangelical world view needs evangelistic focus.

4

Spirituality as a Barrier to Evangelism

What is spirituality? Carrying a worn Bible and passing out tracts on the commuter train? Conducting outdoor street meetings at a suburban mall and seeing Walt Disney movies only? Supernatural without natural, soul without body, sacred without secular? How can evangelism be spiritual and natural at the same time? How can I be me, without part of me being shrunk to the size of a manageable family-skeleton-in-the-evangelism-closet?

One-Dimensional Spirituality

At least two definitions of spirituality today actually reduce Christianity's evangelistic dimensions to merely one. World-centered spirituality considers bodies without souls, and soul-centered spirituality considers souls without bodies. The one puts signs up on its front lawn: "A spirit without a body is a spook." The other decorates its front door entrance with the words "A body without a spirit is a corpse." Both are guilt of reshaping "Christian service," one into a framework as large as the world, the other into a framework as small as a prayer list on a 3x5 card pasted on the bathroom mirror.

World-centered spirituality is a one-dimensional call for

Evangelism: Doing Justice and Preaching Grace

an end to the war between Christianity and secularization. Harvey Cox, the high priest of the movement, insists that secularization is not the enemy of the gospel but its fruit. The secular city *is* the city of God. The old definition of spirituality asked, "Where is God that I may follow Him?" World-centered spirituality asks, "Where is my neighbor, that I may love him?"

In world-centered spirituality, the lines between the church and the world are erased. So the theme of the Second Assembly of the World Council of Churches (1954) is changed from "Christ the Hope of the Church and the World" to "Christ the Hope of the World." For the same reason, the New Delhi Assembly of that same council (1961) removed the word "our" from the phrase "our Lord Jesus Christ" in its constitution. "Our" might appear to be too restrictive, setting the church off from the world.

World-centered spirituality is not simply calling for Christians to get involved. Nor is it simply saying, "If you're not involved, you're not Christian." It says, "If you are involved, you are Christian." World-centered spirituality does not pray, "Thy will be done on earth as it is in heaven." It prays, "Thy will be done on earth, your heaven." It calls us to close all escape hatches from this world into any other world, whether we call it heaven or nirvana. According to this form of one-dimensional spirituality, all we have is the here and now. The secular is the only sacred we can ever know.

On the other end of the one-dimensional spectrum is soul-centered spirituality. Many evangelicals have contented themselves with this. World-centered spirituality asks, "What does spirituality mean to a person paid inadequate wages and renting a rat-infested tenement room?" Soul-centered spirituality asks, "What do inadequate wages and renting a rat-infested tenement room mean to a person when his soul is saved?" One defines spirituality in terms of this-worldliness, the other in terms of other-worldliness; one by sanctifying revolution, the other by sanctifying the status quo. Both are one-dimensional. World-centered spirituality lives by the present tense, in the here and now;

58

soul-centered spirituality lives by the future tense, in the soon coming. One says, "Look down"; the other, "Look up." One defines spiritual in terms of the material, the other in terms of the non material; one in terms of the visible, the other in terms of the invisible.

Both systems withdraw the evangelist from the real world, his field of encounter. One reduces our "warfare with the principalities and powers of evil" to something less than a spiritual one, a vocation but without God, withdrawal from the system but without the God-quest. When he was in solitary confinement, Eldridge Cleaver read Thomas Merton's *Seven Storey Mountain* and speaks for secular man in his frustration: "I was tortured by that book because Merton's suffering, in his quest for God, seemed all in vain to me. . . . All the gods are dead except the god of war. I wished that Merton had stated in secular terms the reasons he withdrew from the political, economic, military and social system into which he was born, seeking refuge in a monastery."[1] Merton had divorced the world from the spiritual, and Cleaver asks him only to be consistent.

Soul-centered spirituality also makes one's contact with society indirect. As Vernon Grounds analyzes the position, the gospel message is seen as only "incidentally social in its application and outworking."[2] This abstraction produces compartmentalization, a spirituality that is less than a whole-world life system and therefore less than fully God-centered. It is this compartmentalization that turns Brazilian university students from Christ to Marx. "You Protestants," they explain, "seem to be concerned only about getting people to stop smoking, drinking and dancing. When the communists speak to us they talk about feeding the starving, teaching the illiterate, and putting an end to exploitation and injustice."[3]

It is this compartmentalization that turns the American black community against the kind of Christianity that speaks of spirituality from the pulpit of a segregated house of worship. Against this one-dimensional Christianity, Malcolm X rebelled in his early career as a minister of Islam. And, in rejecting it, he rejected Christ with it. He wrote:

Evangelism: Doing Justice and Preaching Grace

> Our white slavemaster's Christian religion has taught us black people here in the wilderness of North America that we will sprout wings when we die and fly up into the sky where God will have for us a special place called heaven. This is the white man's Christian religion used to *brainwash* us black people. . . . This blue-eyed devil has *twisted* his Christianity, to keep his *foot* on our backs . . . to keep our eyes fixed on the pie in the sky and heaven in the hereafter . . . while *he* enjoys *his* heaven right *here* . . . on this *earth* . . . in this *life*.[4]

It is soul-centered spirituality that Douglas Johnson and George Cornell may be describing in their book, *Punctured Preconceptions*. In a survey of 3,454 members of the church in North America, they asked them what they thought to be the local church's main task. From a list of fourteen categories, the paramount task was seen as evangelism— "winning others to Christ." Runing a close second to this was "providing worship for members." Midway in the list was "serving as social conscience to the community."[5] "Most people," comment the pollsters, "do regard the church as a personal center of comfort, reassurance and refuge."[6] The gap between "winning others to Christ" and "serving as social conscience" may be there because of soul-centered spirituality.

Two-Dimensional Spirituality

Seeking to avoid the one-dimensional concern for body without soul and the one-dimensional concern for soul without body, many of today's evangelicals write books calling for a "social conscience" that begins with the new birth and "responds positively to society as it is." Jesus' redemptive program is seen to have a social dimension, something frequently missing in the evangelicals' recent past.

The answer to that lost chord is said to be an added dimension, a subscription to *Christianity Today* as well as to the *Christian Century*, a platform that will combine the best of two worlds—the liberal's "horizontal" obligation to love and serve neighbor and the conservative-evangelical's "vertical" obligation to God. Polarization must be resolved

60

in emerging commonality. The Christian is called to obey two mandates—the cultural (Gen. 1:28) and the evangelistic (Matt. 28:18–20). In the past, world-centered spirituality has been too one-dimensional in its Old Testament, prophetic emphasis on "the cultural mandate." And soul-centered spirituality has been too one-dimensional in its New Testament, gospel emphasis on the "evangelistic mandate." The two dimensions must correct each other, with the primary emphasis on the evangelistic mandate.

The Lausanne Covenant, formulated at the 1974 Lausanne Congress on World Evangelization, represents to some degree this two-dimensional spirituality. It properly views evangelism as "the proclamation of the historical, biblical Christ as Saviour and Lord, with a view to persuading people to come to him personally and so be reconciled to God." And it expresses "penitence both for our neglect and for having sometimes regarded evangelism and social concern as mutually exclusive."[7] Both aspects of the gospel are seen as necessary expressions of our Christian duty—our love for our neighbor, and our obedience to Jesus Christ. At the same time, the Covenant says, "In the church's mission of sacrificial service evangelism is primary."[8]

That word *primary* remains for many a piece of undigested two-dimensionalism in the throat of the Lausanne Covenant. It prompted an ad hoc response at Lausanne on "Theology and Implications of Radical Discipleship" by those who wanted a more integral perspective and who felt it was not in keeping with the general thrust of the Lausanne statement. The previous paragraph five of the Covenant speaks of a commitment to the whole of the Christian message, which includes both evangelism and social action. And the sentence immediately following the disputed one reads, "World evangelization requires the whole church to take the whole Gospel to the whole world."

The dispute continues. In June, 1980, more than eight hundred Christians met in Pattaya, Thailand, for the Lausanne-sponsored Consultation on World Evangelization. Again, a grass roots movement drew up a statement of concerns signed by nearly two hundred participants and consultants. In part, the statement read:

> The Lausanne Movement, if it is to make a lasting and profound evangelistic impact in the six continents of the world, must make a special effort to help Christians, local churches, denominations and mission agencies to identify not only people groups, but also the social, economic and political institutions that determine their lives and the structures behind them that hinder evangelism."[9]

Debate on the statement was done behind closed doors and by only a few of those present.[10] The official Thailand statement, *Our Commitment to Christ*, however, seeks no final resolution on the issue but continues to call for balance. Point two of the statement pledges "to work for the evangelization of the world, and to bear witness by word and deed to Christ and his salvation." It is followed immediately by point three and a pledge "to serve the needy and the oppressed, and in the name of Christ to seek for them relief and justice." The evangelical understanding of evangelism, social commitment, and spirituality has taken a dramatic, helpful turn from that of one-dimensionalism.

But the fact remains that we are far from a holistic solution that integrates the two components. The debates that continue to erupt at Lausanne and Pattaya seem to indicate that. Formerly the emphasis was on either body or soul, church or society, evangelism or social action. Now it is on both body and soul, church and society, evangelism and social action. Two abstractions do not make a whole. But two are better than one.

The abstractions remain in much evangelical thinking. They are hidden in statements like, "Nothing could be more disastrous for the church and its witness in the world than for it to give the impression that it is primarily concerned with the needs of the body—economic, social, and political" and, "The mission of the church is preeminently spiritual—that is, its major concern revolves around the nonmaterial aspects of life."

Spirituality as a Barrier to Evangelism

The abstractions remain because of a radical misunderstanding of the dimensions said to be embraced. World-centered spirituality is no more a prophet's corrective for a soul-centered evangelist's lack of balance than New Testament grace is the antidote to Old Testament Sinai thunder. World-centered spirituality has rejected the cultural mandate just as it has rejected the evangelistic mandate. The mandate has been retooled from a call to make the earth fruitful for God's glory to a welfare mandate and a call to make the earth man's kingdom by political means. How can that provide what one evangelical missiologist has called "a necessary corrective" to the evangelical "concern with evangelism and missions"?

And, in the same way, soul-centered spirituality has reduced the evangelistic mandate to something less than Matthew 28:18–20, to a spiritual, nonmaterial mission that cannot be "primarily concerned with the needs of the body." How can that provide a necessary corrective to the liberal concern with social justice and political action? Its very definition has ruled itself out of the arena of combat.

There is a relation between cultural mandate and "great commission" mandate. But it is not an either/or, not a both/and, not even simply a primary/secondary. As John M. L. Young has seen it, Genesis 1:28 is a covenant mandate, the Creator's first proclamation of His mission for His image-bearer. It is more than an isolated mandate governing man's body-life. It is the Sovereign's covenant stipulation for covenant life. That covenant demand still stands, as surely as the curse for breaking the covenant still stands (Gen. 2:17). Only it is now grace that must meet its own demands. And grace has a name—Jesus, crucified, risen and possessing "all authority in heaven and earth." The so-called "missionary mandate" is the covenant mandate's anticipated fulfillment in redemptive grace. They are not basically two mandates but two stages in God's covenant relationship with man. In one, God speaks to covenant man of covenant obligation. In the other, God speaks to covenant breaker of covenant restoration in Christ.[11]

Evangelism: Doing Justice and Preaching Grace

Fourth-Dimensional Spirituality

It is this covenant dimension, this "fourth dimension," that integrates natural and supernatural to the point of questioning even the legitimacy of these terms. To be interested in things spiritual is not to be interested in things nonmaterial/supernatural/invisible/sacred as opposed to things material/natural/visible/secular. To be interested in things spiritual is to be interested in all of life, now touched by the healing hand of the Holy Spirit. It is to be interested in the things that interest the Lord, to have our hearts broken by the things that break the heart of God.

God's interests cannot be programed for action into sacred or "spiritual" categories. God-centered spirituality proclaims the supernatural God who created the natural world in six days and pronounced not only a covenant benediction ("it was good") on each work of each day (Gen. 1:4, 10, 12, 18, 21, 25) but also a special covenant benediction ("it was very good") on it all. The heavens and the earth, what we call "the natural half of reality," are dignified by God as covenant witnesses (Ps. 19:1ff.; Rom. 1:20). They are witnesses to what the earth is designed to be: the garden of God (Ezek. 28:13), where the Creator meets His creature in fellowship. Adam's fellowship with God was to be shown in his earthly, material activity, his subduing rule over nature (Gen. 1:28). That is true spirituality. It totally integrates the spiritual and the physical to the point that the distinction is meaningless.

Adam's fall into sin (Gen. 3) was so deep that it cut a chasm not only between himself and God (Gen. 3:10, 15) but also between himself and nature (3:18–19), between himself and his fellow creatures (3:12–13). Redemptive healing by God is indirectly promised in Genesis 3:15, a healing that will eradicate all the chasms it has cut—with God, with man, and with creation. Cultural mandate, as an expression of the divine purpose for Adam and his seed in the covenant of life, must await the day of integration for an end to its fragmentation, the day of new beginnings for its fulfillment in Christ. The evangelical mandate, God's covenant-of-grace call to discipling the nations, the work of Christ's Spirit in creating the new life of the kingdom come (John 3:3, 5), is the means for that integration, that fulfillment. It is no more two mandates than it is two ways of salvation. It is simply a call to grace, God's response to man's sin that man may fulfill God's call to culture building. God-centered spirituality calls people neither to be hermits nor political lobbyists, but messengers of the Lord's Word both in the church and in the world.

This refusal to see a dichotomy between things spiritual and things material is reflected in God's dealings with Israel. Redemption, as a part of biblical vocabulary, was coined in the victory procession of God's people from Egypt across the Red Sea to Sinai. "Let my people go" was more than a call of God to save merely souls.

And it was this refusal to separate spiritual from material that made Amos storm into Bethel, thundering about the day when the Lord would send, not charity, not compassion, but justice: "Let justice roll on like a river, and righteousness like a never-failing stream" (Amos 5:24).

It was against people who did divide their "spiritual" habits of prayer from their "material" habits of real-estate profiteering (Isa. 5:8–9) and discrimination against minorities (Isa. 1:23; Jer. 5:28) that God spoke through Isaiah: "What do you mean by crushing my people and grinding the faces of the poor?" (Isa. 3:15). God's final Year of Jubilee (Lev. 25) was coming. It would bring good news for the afflicted, healing for the broken hearted, liberty for the captives, freedom for the prisoners (Isa. 61:1ff.). It would be a time of the Lord's favor, a "day of salvation" when God would finally and fully help (Isa. 49:8; 2 Cor. 6:2), a day of restoration, a day to "rebuild the ancient ruins, and restore the places long devastated" and to "renew the ruined cities" (Isa. 61:4; Acts 15:13–18). God's great society, His Age of Aquarius, the welfare program of the Messiah, would make the wrongs right, turn ashes into garlands and mourning into the oil of gladness.

All this would happen when the Spirit came. The Lord

65

would send the Savior anointed for this task of kingdom restoration. And the Spirit of the Lord God would be on Him to do it (Isa. 61:1). "The Spirit of the Lord will rest on him" and "with righteousness he will judge the needy, with justice he will give decisions for the poor of the earth" (Isa. 11:2, 4). "Here is my servant," says the Lord, "I have put my Spirit on him and he will bring justice to the nations" (Isa. 42:1). True spirituality would be the mark of the Messiah and the Messiah's people. With it would come God's new deal for His creation.

The good news that turns Old Testament into New Testament is that the day of "Spirit-uality" has begun. It has begun because its inaugurator has come, the One whose virgin birth is so intimately related to the Holy Spirit (Luke 1:35), the One whose coming puts a new phrase on the lips of the gospel writer seeking to explain the new wind blowing. "Filled with the Holy Spirit" becomes the new phrase that identifies the people of the New Day—such as John the Baptist (Luke 1:15), Elizabeth (1:41), Zacharias (1:67), and Simeon (2:25). The One who will baptize in the Holy Spirit (Luke 3:16; Acts 1:5) is Himself baptized in the Spirit (Luke 3:22), anointed for messianic office. In initial fulfillment of that office, Jesus "full of the Holy Spirit . . . was led by the Spirit in the desert, where for forty days he was tempted by the devil" (4:1–2). He returned from that temptation "in the power of the Spirit" (4:14) and carried on His messianic work of kingdom healing and evangelism, conscious that God's jubilee year of salvation had come "in the power of the Spirit" (4:17–21). Under the Spirit's direction, He went to Jerusalem where He was to be put to death for sinners "but made alive by the Holy Spirit" (1 Peter 3:18; cf. Rom. 8:11).

This new day of the Spirit has everything to do with social involvement. Mary joyfully cried, "My soul praises the Lord and my spirit rejoices in God my Savior. . . . he has brought down rulers from their thrones but has lifted up the humble. He has filled the hungry with good things but has sent the rich away empty" (Luke 1:46, 52–53). In the words of Sherwood E. Wirt, Mary knew that the Lord God was on the verge of doing great things. The system must go. The redeemer and deliverer of Israel was knocking at the door of history. Let the sons of Herod tremble. Let the keepers of empire beware. God was about to undo the work of power-hungry men and to give the earth back to his people. He would somehow liquidate the arrogant military and economic oppressors.[12]

At Calvary, Jesus united evangelism with His work of restoring society. He broke the chains that shackled the world's cultures to their own sins; justice and mercy meet and kiss each other at the blood-sprinkled throne of grace we call Golgotha. By faith the world is called to join in the glorious liberty of the children of God. The beginning of the end has come, the previews of coming attractions when God will finally and perfectly restore "a new heaven and a new earth, the home of the just" (2 Peter 3:13). The work of re-creation in Christ (2 Cor. 5:17) is the start of God's great society, which He will complete at glory when Jesus comes again. Jesus, the "lamb, looking as if it had been slain" (Rev. 5:6), died not to restore a secular city but to bring 'down out of heaven' from God the New Jerusalem." Nothing impure will ever enter it, nor will anyone who does what is shameful or deceitful, but only those whose names are written in the Lamb's book of life" (Rev. 21: 2, 27).

But, in the meantime, what? As the people of the Spirit, baptized in the Spirit (Acts 1:5; 2:1–4; 1 Cor. 12:13), what is our calling in the world while Christ tarries? When Paul says that we "are controlled not by the sinful nature but by the Spirit" (Rom. 8:9), is he telling us that we should not be concerned about questions like politics, police, or poverty? When Paul contrasts "the man without the Spirit" with "spiritual man" (1 Cor. 2:14), is he defining an evangelist with the "extra plus" that separates him from the ordinary, run-of-the-mill Christian? When one is in the Spirit (Rom. 7:6; 8:9; 1 Cor. 12:3), is he thereby out of everything else but testimonies and twenty-minute Bible studies at lunch hour?

Rather, it is the opposite. To "live according to the sinful nature" (Rom. 8:5) is abnormal. It means to live outside of Christ (cf. Gal. 5:16ff.). "Sin nature" or "flesh" is Paul's epigram for life in hostility to Christ, life under the curse of the law, life in sin. To be "in the Spirit" is to be under the domination of the Holy Spirit, to be the organ through which the Spirit expresses Himself (1 Cor. 12:3).

Lewis B. Smedes writes, "Spirit and flesh are both shorthand for the whole situation which each dominates. Being in the Spirit means being in the new situation, created by Christ and dominated by His Spirit."[13] It means living in the day of new beginnings because Christ has come. It means living by faith in a new relationship, with a new disposition, because of a new vitality—all this because the Holy Spirit has come and is doing His initiating work of the new creation in our lives.

This kind of spirituality does not equip us for evangelism by taking us out of the world. It puts a new world into us, the world of the spiritual, that new lifestyle caused by the Holy Spirit, centered in the Holy Spirit, and possessed by the Holy Spirit. It is not an inner work, as opposed to an outer work. As Geerhardus Vos puts it, "There has been created a totally new environment, or more accurately stated, a totally new world. . . . The whole surrounding world has assumed a new aspect and a new complexion. . . ."[14] The creative center is the Cross. The dominant person is the Holy Spirit. The arena is history. The Christian is a new person, living in a new world. Living in the Spirit is not an evangelistic escape from history, but a participation in the new reality of history brought by the redemptive work of Christ and the applying work of the Holy Spirit.

For this reason the New Testament letters are filled with discussions of the spiritual life that interweave the heralding of the good news with topics like racial intolerance, the eating of foods used in pagan ceremonies, the position of women, family relationships, prostitution, homosexuality, the relief of poverty. To equate the spiritual with the nonphysical is completely unintelligible by New Testament standards. To isolate evangelism from the context of the world's concerns emasculates the one and ignores the other.

In this "spiritual life" there are new weapons for changing the world. The War Lord of the universe did not enter Jerusalem on a charger but on a donkey (Zech. 9:9). And He gives to His people for rule, not a scepter, but a towel (John 13:12–15). The power of Rome is destroyed, not by war, but by the phrase "Jesus is Lord." Our weapons against social injustice, government corruption, racial slur, and ghetto hatred are the fruit of the Spirit—love, joy, peace, patience, kindness, goodness, faithfulness, gentleness, self-control (Ga. 5:22–23).

Where will this view of the spiritual life and of evangelism take us? In Sioux Falls, South Dakota, it led the First Baptist Church to begin a halfway house where men released from prison could live for a nominal rent until they could get jobs. Leighton Ford relates a poignant story of the effects of loving concern: "One parolee in his thirties had been in reform school or prison every year since his mid-teens. One day as he sat in the living room, the three-year-old daughter of the couple in charge crawled up in his lap, put her arms around his neck, and gave him a hug. With tears rolling down his cheeks, he said, 'You know, this is the first time I can remember anybody touching me in love.' A few weeks later that man publicly expressed his commitment to Jesus Christ as Lord and Saviour."[15]

In the summer of 1980 I joined four whites and several Ugandan brothers on the garbage piles of Kampala. Nine years under Idi Amin had left the city devastated by terror, its public-health facilities paralyzed. There were massive piles of garbage on almost every corner of the city of over 800,000. Children climbed over the piles, throwing stones at the rats. Every street told the same story. We asked ourselves, "What can we do to dramatize God's love for the city and our willingness to serve in humility?" Jack Miller gave the answer, and "garbage evangelism" was born.

We visited the Minister of Health asking for the use of his trucks to haul away the garbage. He couldn't believe us.

69

Evangelism: Doing Justice and Preaching Grace

"Why?" he kept asking. "Jesus," we answered. He personally escorted us to the parking area where the trucks were kept. Over 150 trucks were there, but only two were usable. Amin had taken the wheels off most of them for use in his war machine.

On the trucks we raised our banners that proclaimed, "Jesus Is the Answer" as we rumbled through the city streets to the great garbage piles near the city markets. Two days a week the cycle began—long days of smelling refuse and filth and singing gospel songs as we worked. Literally hundreds of people circled the piles as we worked and sang. During our breaks we preached the gospel by the piles, with lots of "earthy" illustrations covering theological topics such as total depravity and the grace of God. A newspaper reporter interviewed us. "Why are you doing this?" he asked. From onlookers came similar questions. "Are you members of a political party?"

One of our sharper theological students answered, "Yes, we're citizens of the kingdom of God."

"Which party is that? I've never heard of that party." He soon learned.

Waldron Scott, former General Secretary of the World Evangelical Fellowship, pointed out at the Pattaya Consultation that the 75 percent of the people of the world who are unreached by the gospel are by and large the poor people of the earth. How can we continue our evangelistic apartheid?

As the spiritual pilgrims march, they are in agony. It is the agony of people who know that the new day of the Spirit has come and that the world does not believe. It is the agony of people who know that the Spirit has come to initiate the final day of perfect justice and justification and that injustice and sin still remain. It is the agony of people who know that the "new exists wherever Christ is known, confessed and served as the Lord of life."[16] And yet many still wear rags and hunt for scraps on the garbage heaps of the world.

The old age still claims its captive slaves. Even though the god of this age has been defeated by the risen Christ, those in Christ often see so little in society that indicates the radical righteousness and love characteristic of the new creation. So the spiritual ones continue to pray and to agonize with their brothers under the altar: "How long, O Lord?" (Rev. 6:9).

5

Prayer: Where Word and Deed Come Together

Christians today increasingly find themselves forced to choose between evangelism and engagement in social action. And within the evangelical community too frequently it is a choice for evangelism. Richard Mouw relates how one man expressed it in a recent conversation: "I suppose that there is some room for Christians to wrestle with social issues. But that's not my choice. I see my calling as one of engaging in evangelism. I'll spend my time winning souls for Christ; social action is something I'll leave to the liberals."[1]

The Christian who spoke those words was conceding some place for social action, but he identified it with the liberal cause and not with his. He was doing much more than simply affirming his individual gifts for service in the body. He was also questioning the legitimacy of those who have decided their gifts must be exercised in areas of social ministry. He made his choice in a context of evangelism over against social commitment.

The argument of this book has been that evangelism must involve both verbal witness and exemplary deeds. The "simple" gospel is a very full gospel indeed. You cannot avoid social questions when you are witnessing to prostitutes in Korea about Jesus Christ. What will you do with these young women if they are ready then and there to begin their pilgrimage in Christ? And shouldn't something be done to stop the women from entering this form of temporary slavery in the first place? Where does the gospel end and where does it begin?

What will evangelism say and do among the Karamojong people of northeastern Uganda? In June 1980, says one reporter for the *New York Times*, "a traveler could take a half-day's drive down any dusty track in Karamoja and pass the bodies of at least 40 boys locked out by their families the night before." The weekly death rate then was a hundred or more. Where does the gospel end and where does it begin on dusty tracks like that?

Is there a place where all these concerns merge, where social action will not catch laryngitis and evangelism's extended cup of cold water in the name of Jesus will not be crippled by paralysis? The answer to our tendency to be one-sided and short-sighted, the answer to the energy crisis of the spirit, is *prayer*. Prayer's asking is not wishing. It is demanding that people come to Christ because Christ has come to us. It is demanding that the world be changed because Christ has come to change it.

How to Recognize the Dawning of the New Day

Why has prayer lost this central place as the crossroads of evangelism in word and deed? Why does it have a way of floating away from the center, of becoming peripheral? Because we have confined prayer to that neat little compartment of "housekeeping projects" known as the devotional life, the schizophrenic bungalow around the back of what Daniel Poling has spoken of as "the biggest buildings-and grounds, construction-and-shrubbery-trimming period of Christian history." Because we have made prayer simply a pragmatic exercise based on the practice of Jesus—"Jesus prayed and so should we." We have lost the shattering place of prayer in the history of redemption. Jesus entered the new age of prayer, and we enter with Him and after Him.

Prayer: Where Word and Deed Come Together

Luke in particular draws attention to the gaps in our theology of prayer. In his two-volume story of the words and works of Jesus, he gives prayer its theological place in the divinely directed cosmic plan of salvation. Thirty-four of the eighty-four occurrences of the most common verb for prayer in the New Testament, *proseuchomai*, are in Luke's writings.

Many scholars have noted the uniqueness of Luke's account of the prayer life of Jesus.[2] Luke speks of nine prayers of Jesus, seven of which are not mentioned by the other gospel writers. Luke alone tells us that Jesus was praying in Caesarea Philippi and asked his disciples, "Who do the crowds say I am?" (9:18). Luke alone tells us that Jesus took Peter, James, and John up to the mount to pray when he was transfigured (9:28–29). Luke alone records the request of Jesus' disciples: "Lord, teach us to pray, just as John taught his disciples" (11:1). Luke alone tells the prayer parables of the friend at midnight asking for bread (11:5–8) and the shameless widow begging the judge (18:1–8). Luke alone notes Jesus' prayer for Peter that when Satan wanted to "sift" him, his faith would not fail (22:31–32). And only Luke records Jesus' exhortation to the disciples to pray on their arrival at Gethsemane (22:40).

But though writers often point out the attention Luke gives to Jesus' prayers, few delve into the reason for this emphasis. They cut the line connecting Luke's portrait of Jesus as the Messiah, the great evangelist, the inaugurator of the kingdom day for the poor, and prayer. Luke's account of the prayer life of Jesus and His people cannot be fully understood apart from Luke's approach to the history of divine salvation. He understands the prayer of Jesus as a reminder that a new page has been turned in God's dealing with people. Jesus, the anointed of the Spirit, enters as forerunner into the Age of the Spirit, and his life of prayer mainfests this act of entering in. He prays "through the Holy Spirit" (Luke 10:21). Prayer becomes God's eschatological link between the beginning of the fulfillment and its consummation in glory.

This perspective on prayer is a great feature of the Old

Testament prophets, who describe the time of the coming kingdom as a time of answered prayer. Isaiah had told Israel that God would hear their prayers no longer (Isa. 1:15). "Your iniquities have separated you from your God; your sins have hidden his face from you, so that he will not hear" (59:2). This is much more than a divine reminder of the prerequisite of personal moral purity for answered prayer. God's people, he was saying, were no longer displaying the lifestyle of a kingdom of priests. So God was going to send them a true priest. And when He came, there would be a new beginning to our world and to our prayer life.

God is going to visit His people as He did in the Garden of Eden. And this time, His people will call, and He will answer (Isa. 58:9). God is going to "create new heavens and a new earth. The former things will not be remembered, nor will they come to mind" (65:17). In this new paradise, the wolf and the lamb will graze together, lions will eat straw, and God says of His people, "Before they call I will answer, while they are still speaking I will hear" (65:24).

In the new heavens and earth, all will pray and worship the Lord. Foreigners who join themselves to the Lord will be brought to God's holy mountain. The center of that joy will be God's house of prayer, which "will be called a house of prayer for all people" (Isa. 56:6–7). The last book of the Old Testament sounds the note of the coming great day of prayer. "My name will be great among the nations, from the rising to the setting of the sun. In every place incense and pure offerings will be brought to my name" (Mal. 1:11).

According to Luke, that great day of redemption has dawned, and Jesus, the captain of our salvation, has first entered in as the new Adam. The door opens with prayer. So the opening two chapters of Luke's Gospel are divine talk-shows in which these themes converge: the new age come, a door to the Gentiles opened, God's rearrangement of the social order initiated, prayers offered. While the people stand at prayer outside (1:10), the angel speaks to Zechariah of the coming of the Lord of the new day. Mary sings her battlefield prayers to God in praise of the One who has come to put down the mighty and raise up the poor (1:46–55). Zechariah is described in Luke's eschatological shorthand phrase as "filled with the Holy Spirit" (1:67), and his prayer becomes prophecy, his prophecy prayer: "Blessed be the Lord God of Israel" (1:68). Simeon takes the baby empire-builder in his arms, sees all the nations at His cradle, and prays (2:29–32). Anna sees God's salvation "and she gave thanks to God" (2:38). The Old Testament flavor of these opening chapters moves from a textbook history approach to front-page newspaper journalism, as we participate in God's unfolding drama of the cosmos.

We first read of prayer in the life of Jesus at his baptism. While He was praying (3:21), the Holy Spirit came like a dove to mark the opening of the final page in God's history book, just as a dove had marked another eschatological beginning with Noah (Gen. 8). The heavens were opened—a signal of the beginning of the final dialogue between God and man, and Jesus was anointed for the beginning of the new covenant, the day of prayer for all people.

Jesus was then led by the Spirit into the wilderness for forty days. He entered as the last Adam, a reality to which Luke draws special attention by carefully placing His genealogy between the baptism and the wilderness histories—a genealogy that ends climactically with the words "the son of Adam, the son of God" (3:23–39). Jesus entered the wilderness as the "chosen one," the elect one (Isa. 42:1). Israel had received her testing for forty years under the leadership of Moses. Now Christ, as the new Moses, was tested. Would it be paradise lost or regained? Again the context of the whole messianic struggle is the context of prayer.

Twelve apostles were chosen to proclaim the healing power of the kingdom "here and now," to proclaim blessing to the poor "here and now" because theirs is the kingdom of God (Luke 6). Luke tells us that before He made the appointments "Jesus went into the hills to pray, and spent the night praying to God" (6:12). Jesus' evangelistic mission was not simply undergirded with prayer; it was to be identified with prayer.

At Caesarea Philippi, He revealed to His disciples in a clearer way than ever before His imminent death and resurrection in its relation to His messianic purposes. And all this began, says Luke, while He was praying (9:18). In the same way, Luke records that the experience on the Mount of Transfiguration—where Jesus conversed with Elijah and Moses about "his departure, which he was about to bring to fulfillment at Jerusalem"—came about as Jesus was praying (9:29–31).

The final cycle of prayer comes now where we should expect it—at the place where all the Gospels draw us, the place of Jesus' kingdom-enthronement, His death and resurrection. Luke alone tells us that Jesus was strengthened by an angel in the garden in preparation for His coming judgment-salvation ordeal. And Luke tells us that in prayer He gave up His soul as an offering for sin to the Father (22:39–46) and that two of the three last words of Jesus on the cross are prayers (23:34, 46). Hebrews 5:7 adds the note that through His prayer He was raised from the dead: "During the days of Jesus' life on earth, he offered up prayers and petitions with loud cries and tears to the one who could save him from death, and he was heard because of his reverent submission."

At this point Luke reinforces the link between Jesus at prayer and his contemporary church at prayer. For he has a second volume, the Acts of the Apostles, to write his history of all that Jesus, through the Spirit, did and taught (Acts 1:1). Jesus entered the new age of the Spirit in prayer. Now His people enter that age after Him. The same characteristic of the new age marks them as well, these people who "joined together constantly in prayer" (1:14). The last verses of the Gospel had centered in a climax of prayer and praise (Luke 24:52–53). In the opening verses of Acts the center is still prayer. Only now it is inauguration, not climax. And it is Jesus's people at prayer, and Jesus through them.

"Through prayer" a replacement for Judas was appointed

Prayer: Where Word and Deed Come Together

to the ministry of the apostolate (1:24). "After praying," the church set apart the seven and initiated the ministry of waiting on tables (6:6). After fasting and prayer, the church at Antioch sent Barnabas and Saul to fulfill Christ's commission (13:2–3). Elders were appointed in the struggling new churches of Asia Minor "with prayer and fasting" (14:23).

Just as Jesus manifested the kingdom blessings of salvation and forgiveness of sins, the blessings of the new day of new prayer, so also the church manifested those same kingdom blessings in that same new day of prayer. Paul and Silas proclaimed the kingdom blessing of salvation to the Philippian jailor at midnight, and they prefaced their evangel of the kingdom with prayer and singing in the prison (16:25). Jesus announced the coming of the kingdom through His mighty signs of healing, giving sight to the blind, restoring life to the dead. The early church announced the same kingdom, come in Christ and coming in Christ, through those same mighty signs. Peter prayed in kingdom-power anticipation, and the dead Tabitha arose (9:40). Paul prayed and the sick were healed (28:8). As Jesus had come in prayer "to proclaim freedom for the captives," so the early church's vigil of prayer brought freedom to the captive Peter. The kingdom blessing of prisoners set free became reality (12:12).

The new age of the Spirit was to see old men dreaming dreams and young men seeing visions (Acts 2:17). Peter saw a sheet let down from heaven, and Luke tells us it happened when he "went up on the roof to pray" (10:10). Cornelius saw a man in shining garments, who told him to send for Peter. When Peter came, Cornelius told him, "I was in my house praying" (10:30).

Do today's evangelical activists need prayer? How else can we say to the world, "Only Jesus brings radical change"? How else can we avoid what Dennis Clark has called "the aggressive know-it-all do-it-now disease of western Christianity"?

Ronald Sider, a contemporary leader of the evangelical movement, writes of his recent conversations with many younger evangelical activists who, although their theology, work, and leadership are outstanding, nevertheless confess a deep deficiency in their understanding and practice of prayer. . . . When we see a situation that requires action, we find it far more natural to call together a committee and begin mapping out a strategy for action than to anguish before the Lord in extended prayer. By extended prayer, I mean something more than a perfunctory, introductory 30-second prayer while the last persons straggle in to the meeting. How many of us find it easier to keep up with current politics each day than to spend equal time talking to the King?[3]

Who is more naïve? The liberal leaders of what we now call "the social gospel" with their passionate concern for a broken world and their never-ending optimism of how we may rectify it? Or the evangelical who has given up on the world's headaches in favor of a stripped-down form of evangelism reduced to four spiritual laws? Or the evangelical social activist who does not see intercessory prayer as the first and constant component of our "social evangelism"?

How to Pray in the New Day

What should our prayers be like in this new day of the kingdom of God? Power has to be an evident part, the boldness that comes from seeing the power of the kingdom unleashed before people.

The prayer life of the Jews in the days of Christ was missing this note. Joachim Jeremias writes, "God was primarily the king at a distance from his world, and praying was compared with doing homage. Just as a fixed ceremonial had to be observed at court, so too it was with praying. . . . Formulated prayers were predominant. Prayer was in danger of becoming a habit. Casuistry was getting a grip. . . ."[4] Prayer was becoming a piling up of words to gain merit (Luke 18:11–12). "Beware of the teachers of the law," warned Jesus. "They devour widows' houses and for a show make lengthy prayers" (Luke 20:46–47). A rabbinic proverb encouraged this: "Everyone that multiplies prayers is heard." No, said Jesus, "When you pray, do not keep on babbling like pagans, for they think they will be heard because of their many words" (Matt. 6:7).

Jesus taught us how to pray in the new age. The disciples sensed their need: "Lord, teach us to pray, just as John taught his disciples," they said (Luke 11:1). They were not simply impressed with the prayer life of Jesus. Their question reveals far more than simply their failure in learning how to pray, how to use some sort of heavenly telephone. Religious groups in Jesus' day had characteristic prayers. The Pharisees had such prayers, as did the community at Qumran and the disciples of John the Baptist. Jesus' disciples wanted a prayer that would correspond with His message and His work. They wanted to be able to pray as people should pray who were partaking of the kingdom of God and yet waiting for its final fulfillment.

So Jesus taught us how to pray. No longer need we stand in the synagogue, at the close of the service, saying, "Exalted and hallowed be His great name in the world which He created according to His will. May He let His kingdom rule in your lifetime and in your days and in the lifetime of the whole house of Israel, speedily and soon."[5] In the synagogue, a community is praying—a community still completely in the courts of waiting.

No, said Jesus, we no longer simply hope for the promise of God's name to be hallowed. We rejoice that the promise has begun to be fulfilled: the kingdom rule of God has become the kingdom rule of the Son. May there be a realization here and now of the saving gifts and blessings of God—forgiveness of sins (Jer. 31:34; Matt. 18:23) and bread "for the coming day." May there be preservation from the apostasy of the last terrible hour of temptation, present now (John 16:33) but still to come in its fullest sense.

The power of the kingdom of God has been unleashed, power before which demons bow. People are astonished at the word of kingdom power (Matt. 7:28–29). Miracles pour forth, healing, saving kingdom power to answer the doubts of John the Baptist (Luke 7:18–23).

And, in demonstration of the presence of the kingdom, Jesus prayed with new boldness. He was not content with the apparent custom in His day of liturgical prayer three times a day. He spent all night in prayer to God (Luke 6:12). Outside the regular hour of prayer, He called out to His father at Gethsemane at midnight. The kingdom had come and it shattered even pious custom.

That boldness Jesus now commends to His disciples. Geerhardus Vos reminds us that the human response to the open display of the kingdom of God's power is faith.[6] Jesus adds boldness in prayer to that human response. In the face of His coming death, Jesus withered the fig tree and then said, "If you have faith and do not doubt, not only can you do what was done to the fig tree, but also you can say to this mountain, 'Go throw yourself into the sea,' and it will be done. If you believe, you will receive whatever you ask for in prayer" (Matt. 21:21–22). These miracles were for the world of Jesus expressions that pointed to kingdom power. One of the great eschatological events connected with the kingdom was to be the removing of mountains. Isaiah writes, "A voice of one is calling. 'In the desert prepare the way for the LORD; make straight in the wilderness a highway for our God. Every valley shall be raised up, every mountain and hill made low'" (Isa. 40:3–4). The conclusion of one of Isaiah's great Servant Songs is, "I will turn all my mountains into roads" (49:11). Now, says Jesus, even the weakest kind of faith, as tiny as a grain of mustard seed, can have a share in the beginnings of God's final ending. And how? "I tell you the truth, my Father will give you whatever you ask in my name" (John 16:23).

The Book of Acts shows the answers to that kind of prayer. The church devoted itself to prayer (2:42) and "many wonders and miraculous signs were done by the apostles" (2:43). Prayer brought earthquake responses (4:31). Even Simon the magician was awed by its power and tried to buy it (8:18–19). Peter prayed before the dead body of Dorcas, and she lived (9:40). Paul and Silas prayed in prison and "suddenly there was such a violent earthquake that the foundations of the prison were shaken . . ." (16:26). On Malta Paul prayed for the father of Publius lying in bed afflicted with recurrent fever, "and, after prayer, placed his hands on him and healed him" (28:8).

The black church in the United States has repeatedly tapped this power source. In pre-civil War times Harriet Tubman, a former slave, returned so often to the South to help free other slaves that a bounty of forty thousand dollars was placed on her head. The source of her strength, she repeatedly said, was prayer. One friend said of her, "I never met with any person, of any color, who had more confidence in the voice of God, as spoken direct to her soul. She has frequently told me that she talked with God, and He talked with her every day of her life."[7]

The civil-rights movement and the sit-ins of the 1960s flowed out of the kneel-ins. In 1963 Birmingham, Alabama, became a stormy scene of confrontation between police chief Bull Connor, with his police dogs, and those who made a nonviolent quest for humanity. Fire hoses turned on the crowds were no match for the marchers who left church inspired by a continuous flow of song and prayer. On August 28, 1963, a quarter of a million Americans gathered in Washington at the Lincoln Memorial in a massive celebration of victory. The meeting, which caught the eye of the world, was billed as a "prayer pilgrimage." Harold Carter summarizes the effect of the black prayer tradition at work:

> It has been used by Black women to provide hope and the value of freedom in the hearts of their children. Slaves used this tradition to free themselves and to seek the freedom of other slaves left behind. This prayer tradition provided the spiritual strength for the Black community to sustain a nonviolent struggle against segregation and oppression during the civil rights movement. . . . It has proved itself to be a source of power, not locked behind stained-glass windows, but used wherever Black people seek God's will and respond to his way.[8]

This sort of prayer is at once an act of humility and an act of triumph. Uttered in a haystack during a rainstorm by six college students in 1810, it created a great mission board, the American Board of Commissioners for Foreign Missions, and inaugurated the great sweep of North American missions. Rallying Christian forces in England in 1877, prayer reversed the earlier judgment of a Committee of Parliament and, in 1886 it put an end to the state's patronage and supervision of prostitution.[9]

The counterpoint of bold power in our prayer life is humility. And this too flows from the new reality the world faces with Christ's coming. Here also lies the major area of controversy between Jesus and the Pharisees.

For the Pharisees, the kingdom of God was law. "Taking on the yoke of the law" was taking on "the yoke of the kingdom." At the heart of their concept of the kingdom was merit. "If I do this, if I observe that, if I refrain from such and such, God *must* hear me. My righteousness will batter down the walls of heaven. God audits His ledger books and He will reward me exactly according to my debits and my credits." In this atmosphere, prayer found its meaning in the context of merit. Jesus' parable of the Pharisee and the publican underlined this.

To its first hearers, this parable must have seemed shocking, inconceivable. Today we read it as if Jesus is exaggerating a little. But to Jesus' contemporaries, the prayer of the Pharisee was a genuine prayer of thankfulness. God had given him the opportunity and desire to carry out the practical piety of fasting, tithing, and prayer. A first-century prayer very similar to that of the Pharisee is found in the Talmud:

> I thank thee, O Lord, my God, that thou hast given me my lot with those who sit in the seat of learning and not with those who sit at the street corners; for I am early to work, and they are early to work; I am early to work on the words of the Torah, and they are early to work on things of no moment. I weary myself, and they weary themselves; I weary myself and profit thereby, while they weary themselves to no profit. I run and they run; I run towards the life of the Age to Come and they run towards the pit of destruction.[10]

The conclusion of Jesus is that the Pharisee, and not the publican, will never make the kingdom. It is the Pharisee who is running toward the pit of destruction. Why? Because he runs in self-trust, self-congratulation, and in sin—and

he doesn't even know it. By contrast, the God of the kingdom is the God of the despairing, the broken-hearted, the
hopeless. Humility begins here, where the sinner sees not
himself but God in Christ.

The prayers of the kingdom express this humility, this
God-consciousness. Jesus displayed it more than others. As
He stood before the horror of Calvary, His gallows-throne,
He prayed, "Father, if you are willing, take this cup from
me; yet not my will, but yours be done" (Luke 22:42). Here
is the heart of Jesus humbling Himself to death.

And He taught us to pray in the same way, with that
same kingdom humility; "Your will be done on earth as it is
in heaven." May the Lord, we are to plead, smash our
willfulness and exalt His will. May the kingdom righteousness centered in God's rule, the righteousness and justice of
the coming age, be seen even here, even now, today.

In this spirit, the early church elected an apostle. And
they prayed, "Lord, you know everyone's heart. Show us
which of these two you have chosen" (Acts 1:24). Paul, the
blind man, waited in Damascus, his pride in his hard-won
righteousness shattered, his enthusiasm for maintaining an
up-to-date credit rating in the kingdom all gone. And the
Lord told Ananias, "He is praying" (Acts 9:11).

Do we touch here on one of the biggest problems in our
prayer life—the constant pressure to substitute activity for
prayer? Activity is me-centered, prayer is God-centered. Is
there any significance to the fact that immediately after
Luke recorded the story of Mary and busy Martha (in
chapter 10) he introduced the Lord's prayer? B. B. Warfield
warns us:

> Activity is good: surely in the cause of the Lord we should run
> and not be weary. But not when it is substituted for inner
> religious strength. "We cannot get along without our Marthas.
> But what shall we do when, through all the length and breadth
> of the land, we shall search in vain for a Mary? Of course the
> Marys will be as little admired by the Marthas today as of yore.
> "Lord," cried Martha, "dost thou not care that my sister hath
> left me to serve alone?" And from that time to this the cry has
> continually gone up against the Marys that they waste the

precious ointment which might have been given to the poor, when they pour it out to God, and are idle when they sit at the Master's feet.[11]

Is our evangelism a joyful proclamation of what God has done for us or a frantic "workaholic" search for as many scalps for our evangelical belt as we can find? Biblical evangelizing is a twofold commission: to preach and to pray, to talk to people about God and to talk to God about people. The world presses against us. Secularization wipes out boundaries and reduces the sacred to the secular. Prayer, as a means of crossing that boundary, is wiped away with it, reduced to the size of a world big enough for us to handle. Pragmatism forces prayer to compete with doing; technology, endowed with an efficacy in and of itself, refuses to recognize its own uncertainty or insufficiency. "I owe it all to God" has become easy talk and self-justification.[12]

To power and humility we add a third component—intimacy, a new shamelessness. The world of Jesus' day was tongue-tied. God was at a regal distance from the world and could not be addressed except in circumlocution. Prodigal sons could only speak of heaven when they meant God. "Father, I have sinned against heaven and against you" (Luke 15:18). Prayer became cap in hand homage.

Then Jesus came and peacemakers were blessed in the here and now. How? People could begin to call them sons of God (Matt. 5:9). *Father,* an old word on the Hebrew tongue, was given a new lease on life, a new intimacy. In the Old Testament, the fatherhood of God was related to Israel in an unparalleled manner. "Israel is my firstborn son," the Lord told Moses as his warning to Pharaoh (Exod. 4:22). Then Jesus came, and in the uniqueness of the relationship of divine Father to divine Son, he called God "Father." The title is on the lips of Jesus 170 times in the Gospels.

Jesus is Son in a way that no one else is Son. He is intimate in prayer in a way we cannot follow. We cannot pray as He did. Yet He says to us, "When you pray, say:

Prayer: Where Word and Deed Come Together

'Father'" (Luke 11:2). The salvation of God's people would come when God revealed Himself as the sovereign, saving King. Now Jesus says, "Do not be afraid, little flock, for your father has been pleased to give you the kingdom" (Luke 12:32).

How will we approach this heavenly Father? With persistence we can come at midnight and ask for our three loaves (Luke 11:5–6). And the Lord will give, not because He is friend, but because He is Father (Luke 11:11–13).

In the face of injustice and inequity, we come with shamelessness. Didn't God say He would come with justice to judge the poor? Wasn't He to decide with fairness for the afflicted of the earth (Isa. 11:4)? Didn't God promise us there would be a judge in the tents of David: He "seeks justice and speeds the cause of righteousness" (Isa. 16:5). Doesn't Psalm 72:3 exclaim, "He will defend the afflicted among the people, and save the children of the needy; he will crush the oppressor"? Won't the new day of the kingdom be the day when God will be "a father to the fatherless and a defender of widows" (Ps. 68:5)?

Well, we're in the new day of the kingdom. Where is all this justice? Jesus said, "Blessed are those who hunger and thirst for righteousness [for putting things right], for they will be filled" (Matt. 5:6). But the church still looks for the final audit of the world's books. Mother Theresa in Calcutta still ministers to the poor and dying. Racism still taints the streets of New York and London.

Against this world in its fallenness, against this agenda twisted out of its God-center, we are to cry out, widows asking persistently for justice before the "unjust judge" (Luke 18:1–5). The promised recipients of the care, the protection, of the divine Kinsman are not stopped by long delays (18:4). Even those who do not take the justice of God seriously bow before importunate widows who keep calling. Prayer becomes sanctified "rebellion against the status quo."[13] We should always "pray and not give up."

Pray between "the already" of the kingdom come in Christ and the "not yet" of the kingdom still to come in

Evangelism: Doing Justice and Preaching Grace

Christ. We have been waiting for the time when God comes to vindicate His people and do justice. That day has come. But the day of final, full justice still waits for the Lord to return. Until the job is finished by Almighty God, we pray. Until justice rolls down like water, until the earth is covered with the knowledge of God, we keep asking. Until every nation calls him Lord, we keep knocking.

Bringing men and women to Christ in faith and gaining victory over unjust principalities and powers do not come simply, or even primarily, or even to start with, by swamping our senators with letters and petitions, looking for new bandwagons to jump on, holding one more successful church seminar, or joining marches to the Pentagon. Changes begin with petitionary prayer, the elect crying to God day and night about Ireland and massive military spending and Billy Graham Crusades in Minneapolis.

God puts our persistence to the test by not answering us immediately. It seems like such a long time. But He answers "quickly" Quickly is not immediately. Ask any eight-year-old counting the days before the family trip to the zoo.

We will be tempted to give up on prayer. It takes so long, the world moves so slowly, justice seems so far away. "When the Son of man comes, will he find faith on the earth?" (Luke 18:8). Jesus is not offering us some eschatological pessimism here about the state of the Christian faith. He is calling us to faithfulness in unfailing prayer for the manifestation of righteousness. The temptation in petitionary prayer is always to submit, to acquiese to what is, to come to terms with the unjust and unsaved world around us. We lose our anger at the wrongness of what is and lose with it our desire to persevere. We succumb to Doris Day theology: *que será, será*, the situation is unchangeable, what is will always be. No, says God, do not faint. And what is the mark of that confidence that God does build His kingdom of grace and justice? Shamelessness in prayer to the Father.

Those we label liberal have problems with this kind of prayer.

Prayer: Where Word and Deed Come Together

John Robinson wrote honestly, but pathetically, of the increasing difficulties he encountered sustaining a conventional devotional life along with his radical theology. The death-of-God theologians in the 1960s wrote disparagingly about prayer. Paul Tillich declared that, no, he did not pray but he did meditate. And Jürgen Moltmann has declared this is an aspect of "privatized" religion that ought to be jettisoned.[14]

Do evangelicals have a better track record? Our leaders call us increasingly to world challenges as big as all outdoors, but our prayer lists are limited to a new leader for the church youth group, a forthcoming meeting of the trustees, or that obstreperous elder in the congregation. Social change we leave to the politicians, evangelism to the mass campaigns. Where do we leave prayer?

6
Models: How to Change What We've Got

The pastor today is bombarded with countless examples of church growth and models for ministry. He reads of the Thomas Road Baptist Church in Lynchburg, Virginia. Described by Elmer Towns as "the fastest-growing church in America," it began in 1956 with thirty-five adults and children. Its membership grew to over 15,000 within twenty years.

Dan Baumann in his book, *All Originality Makes a Dull Church,* calls the College Church of Northhampton, Massachusetts "the social-action church." It held its first worship service in April 1972. Now the congregation owns seven acres of land and has a morning attendance averaging close to eight hundred. That is the highest average of all Protestant churches in western Massachusetts. Baumann writes:

> Every week hundreds of College Church people are serving Christ in the community. Large crews of volunteers work at the three Northhampton hospitals—a state mental hospital, a VA hospital and the Cooley Dickinson Hospital. Others serve in the five rest homes, providing visitation, services and kindness. One man regularly takes someone from a convalescent home as his personal guest to football and basketball games. After a recent rainstorm, two church members repaired the leaky roof of an elderly couple's home.[1]

Evangelism: Doing Justice and Preaching Grace

The heart of this church's ministry is the breadth of involvement among its members and its identification with the community.

Perhaps you have heard of the Fellowship Bible Church of Dallas, Texas. Started in 1972 and shepherded by Gene Getz of Dallas Theological Seminary, it holds four identical worship services on a weekend with over a thousand people meeting each time. It is committed to a balance of instruction, fellowship, and witnessing.

Do We Need New Models?—Reinvestigation

These examples can draw any number of reactions from us. Let me eliminate two of the worst. There is the sour-grapes response. By it we pray, "God, we thank Thee that we are not like that growing church, drawing people with itching ears. Our people tithe and fast and memorize our creeds."

Equally useless is the bandwagon mentality. It sends pastors on endless quests to one successful church seminar after another in endless attempts to copycat Garden Grove or the First Baptist Church of Dallas in Kalamazoo or Ruston. Too often these quests end in disappointment and frustration months later.

Do we need new models? The 1977 statistical report of one demonination I know is filled with good reasons. Beware of statistics, but at least learn from them. Between 1975 and 1977 this denomination lost a total of nearly 200 church families. Two new churches came into being in 1977. But five merged into two churches and six have been dissolved. Total baptized membership is down 1,609 in one year's time. There were 173 fewer confessions of faith than in 1976, 140 fewer transfers, and 23 fewer adult baptisms. The picture is not untypical of many churches. Do we agree with E. Stanley Jones that our fellowship has many people who "know about God, but don't know Him; are informed about Christ, but are not transformed by Him; who know about the moral laws, but are powerless to fulfill them"?[2]

Dr. Ted Ward of Michigan State University recently

isolated five problems in the church models we build today. I list them as questions for you now and ask you to provide your own answers.

1. *Passivity of the laity.* Have you found yourself saying within the past year, "The people push responsibility onto their pastors. I don't seem to be able to get them motivated to do something"? On some dismal Monday morning, have you confided to your wife, "Do they want *me* or my *car?*"

2. *Hierarchy.* Doesn't the body of Christ today still suffer from the chiefs-and-Indians syndrome? An awful lot of Indians and relatively few chiefs, with the chiefs making most of the decisions? Are we willing to admit that the evangelical churches of today have not really fallen into these structures? They have just never reformed out of it. Did the Reformers, in their struggle with Rome, escape fully enough from the hierarchical structures characteristic of the church of their day? Hendrik Kraemer, in his book *The Theology of the Laity,* says we didn't. Does his answer make you comfortable or uncomfortable?

3. *Intellectual meritocracy.* In the church, says Ward, status is earned by knowing; what is required for leadership is the possession of a "magic bag of merits."

> These magic bags of merit are systematically dealt out only to a relatively few players in the game. The dealers are the theological seminaries. Once a magic bag of merit is in one's possession, it can be traded for honor and prestige (plus a salary) at the friendly local church, and thus one maintains oneself, career and salary, more in terms of what one knows than what one *is.* [3]

The language to many of us may sound extreme. But some hard questions may highlight the problem. Is it not true that the Bible suggests relatively few criteria for the elder or for the pastor that relate to what one knows? Is it not true that our examinations for ordination focus by and large on what information the candidate has gathered and can reproduce with a maximum of ease before his peers? Is there not almost a hidden presumption in most of us that if a ministerial candidate has graduated from Seminary X or

Bible School Y he must be qualified? How deeply is our concept of ordination dictated by what Ward calls the educational establishment?

4. *Pride and status.* Has leadership become something of an end in itself? Have the teachings of Christ about servanthood become culturally clouded by the Horatio Alger syndrome: one begins low in order to become great? How real is the danger in ministry that servanthood becomes a temporary or transient period of initiation or demonstration of eligibility? Is leadership defined too often not by service but by privileges?

5. *Manipulative tactics.* Is the leadership of our churches resorting to manipulative strategies and procedures to move the body forward? Do we too quickly substitute for encouragement through fellowship and vitalization through prayer the manipulation of guilt to get certain kinds of conformity? —guilt about the racial crisis, guilt about the status of women, guilt about the poor? Do we make use of fear? Do we sanctify the technique of manipulative gossip, brainwashing by labels? "Oh, they'll never buy a community ministry; they're fundamentalists. You know how they voted on the homosexual question." Or, "That church has no interest in supporting an evangelistic thrust in our neighborhood; they're liberals. You know how they voted on the homosexual question."

I'm sure there is much truth behind some of these snap judgments, too much for most of us. But I'm also sure this language may betray a hidden call to manipulation, and an impoverished understanding of leadership in the body of Christ.

All these problems in our current models are cyclical. Each feeds on the others and the whole thing keeps coming back to what may be its source—the passivity of the laity. Any church with one or more of them may be a church with all of them. We have just not looked deeply enough to see the rest below the surface. One or all of them are mandates for change. And one or all of them are inhibitors to change. What can we do?

Models: How to Change What We've Got

What Does a Model Do?—Reinforcement

Providing you now with a stirring list of churches that have changed will not help. You can read about them in Peter Wagner's *Your Church Can Grow* (Regal, 1976) or Wendell Belew's *Churches and How They Grow* (Broadman, 1971). The sociological analysis of Lyle Schaller and his volume *Hey, That's Our Church!* (Nashville: Abingdon, 1975), is also a mine of data. I would like now to remind you of what models do for us and to us. As I do, I borrow from a science little used by most of us in our North American churches, that of cultural anthropology.

In 1962 Thomas Kuhn jolted the scientific world with his study of models and paradigms, *The Structure of Scientific Revolutions* (Chicago: University of Chicago Press, 1962). Many things he said can be of help to us in church renewal. Kuhn saw that models have a formative effect on the way we see things. We perceive data in terms of some combination of models that we have been taught and that we have constructed. Through the model, our spectacles, we scale reality down so that we can understand it. The model becomes what he calls a paradigm, "a normative illustration of proper method, of how to handle new as well as old cases and data." The model becomes the gathering place, the testing ground for those principles of order by which we evaluate a cosmos. It is a model of reality, not the real thing. It takes the essential pieces of the real thing and scales them down so that we can understand them.

According to Kuhn, major advances in scientific endeavor happen when scientists shift their models. They shift from one way of viewing their data to another way of viewing it. Our vision is more often obstructed by what we think we know than by our lack of knowledge. For most of us, the easiest illustration of this was the shift from Ptolemaic astronomy to Copernican. That shift is now called the Copernican revolution. Revolution came not with a vast flood of new data, but with a new way of modeling what we had.

What does all this have to do with models of ministry in

the 1980s? Are we aware of how our current models of the church filter out and scale down biblical perspectives on the church? Are we always falling into the temptation of restructuring biblical givens into model demands, not because we do not know what the Bible says but because we do not know how our church paradigm models biblical reality to sociological phenomena?

Recently, Howard Snyder has written about the structure of the church in *The Problem of Wineskins* (Downers Grove: InterVarsity, 1975). There is so much in that book of help to us. One of the most helpful is his charting of the problems.

He fears our tendency to make sacred what he calls the structures of the church and suggests that not only parachurch structures but also denominations may be legitimate and necessary, but neither of these is the church. He does not want to say that no structures themselves are part of the essence of the church. His fears about structure come from our historical tendency to absolutize the institutional shape of the church. My own concerns are very much like his.

I have my concerns with some of the turns his argument seems to take. For example, I fear he does not recognize adequately enough that the church even in the New Testament had a structural shape. The church as the community of God's people, the fellowship of the Spirit, had an institutional and structural form. Charismatic ardor was to be balanced by structural order (1 Cor. 14:40).

But in spite of this criticism of his views, he raises a legitimate, persistent question. How can we escape the dangers he warns us of today—absolutization of structures and overidentification of the way we do things with the way the Spirit intends to do things, confusing man-made, culturally determined forms with Spirit-made, biblically guided freedom? Let us recognize the formative shape of our models on the biblical vision of reality under God. Our models of ministry can change biblical perspective into sociocultural realities. We see the biblical portrait of the church not as it is but always from inside such models.

This came forcefully to my attention in the past few years

Models: How to Change What We've Got

of teaching at Westminster Theological Seminary. I had been asked to teach the senior course on Pastoral Theology until a permanent faculty replacement could be found. In the curriculum sequence that course is preceded by a course on the doctrine of the church, taught by Dr. Edmund Clowney. I had found the material from his course of great help to me in my understanding of world missions. I would not hesitate to call it radical in its impact. And yet now I was teaching pastoral theology and saw little direct influence from it in the shaping of the church's structures. Students had taken Clowney's course for years and yet the churches our alumni planted showed little change or movement. Why?

About this time, in the course of my reading, I discovered Kuhn and cultural anthropology. And a new thought struck me. Were the students doing with their models what Kuhn said was being done by the scientists? Were they filtering the radical materials from that course through the old models and using the data not for innovation but for reinforcement? Were the old models they brought with them to the course shaping what they would receive or not receive from that course on ecclesiology? Was the problem really with their grasp of the new data they had received, or was it with the models through which they filtered the data?

Accordingly I decided to use the course to offer new models. Pastors were invited in to talk about their congregations. Students heard about churches in the suburbs, churches in the inner city, churches with small-group fellowships, churches that used the old patterns in new and dynamic ways. It was not new data that I introduced to them. It was new models. Suddenly the class came alive. Students have come to me on campus and asked, "How can I effect change? Where do I begin?" And they were students no one would call radicals. Now I regularly receive letters from young men in the ministry. And they are working through the same questions that concern me. What effected the change? It was not simply an underlining of biblical information. They had that before they entered the

97

class. It was the reality of that data fleshed out in new models.

How does a model of the church affect our biblical vision? In at least five ways.

1. *All models explain.* They explain how and why things got to be as they are and how and why they continue or change. In so-called primitive culture, myths arise as tools of explanation. In western culture we accomplish much the same with our secularized forms of mythology—science, politics, art. And in Christianity we explain biblical ecclesiology with existing models.

2. *All models evaluate.* Within a culture, the model judges other customs as inferior or at least inappropriate and reaffirms the inherent rightness of its own patterns and modes of expression. Within the church, this tendency inhibits believers from leaving a church where they may feel they are not being fed or where there is no growth. This characteristic may be behind the sentiment sometimes expressed in this way: "I know things are bad. But it was my parents' church. Where would I go?" It also hinders believers from learning new patterns from nearby churches. "Well, sure they're growing. But what do you expect? They're Pentecostal!" I remember vividly a conversation I had with a lay leader from a church in the United States. The church had been there over twenty years and had become captive to an ideological conservatism. In the meantime, the city had moved into a more radical lifestyle, mirroring a large university in the area. Another fellowship equally conservative theologically had started there some years before and had shaped its patterns of worship and structures to meet the new lifestyle. It was now double the size of the older work. But when the leader and I discussed these matters, his only response was a repeated exclamation, "But we're conservative. You can't expect us to shift the pattern of our life just because the community has. After all, the question is, What does God want?" That man was guilty of mistaking an ideology for theology and creating a model for the church that perpetuated not only the theology but the ideology as well.

Models: How to Change What We've Got

3. *All models provide psychological reinforcement for the group.* Within human culture when times of crisis arise, the model reinforces the society's equilibrium. The model provides security and support for the behavior of the group in a world that appears to be out of control. Within the church, this tendency produces its own set of proverbs. It responds to efforts to change by protesting, "But we've never done it that way before." To the threats of a changing neighborhood, it replies, "Maybe we should move to the suburbs." To the possibility of a new focus of ministry on the aged or on youth, it sighs in resignation, "Well, I guess we have to change or we'll go under." The problem here is not lack of concern or even lack of courage. It is the pressure of the church model toward psychological reinforcement. Resisting that pressure alone may bring renewal. Read the August 1978 issue of *Eternity Magazine*. It chronicles the history of a Bethany Church in Mt. Morris, Michigan. You will not find any startling new methods for renewal. It does not even boast of spectacular growth. But it made a decision to stay in a changing neighborhood and is losing its character as a Sunday drop-in center. That decision was crucial enough for the author to comment, "Perhaps it was a miracle." It was most assuredly a vote against psychological reinforcement. And that was the beginning of its break-out.

4. *All models integrate.* They systematize and order their perceptions of reality into an overall design. And they filter out those glimpses of reality that do not conform to their beliefs concerning the way reality should be. The model provides us with a way of clothing our view of perceived realities with factuality. We conceptualize what we think the reality should be and we create the model to integrate the concept.

This also can be an inhibiting factor in renewal. David Mains, in the same issue of *Eternity Magazine* mentioned above, asks the question, "Can my church be changed?" Part of his answer is that "a call to renewal includes a certain nomadic flavor. You live mentally with tent pegs in hand, always aware it may be time to pull up stakes."[4]

That nomadic flavor is resisted by the integrating character of models. This does not mean that renewal is
synonymous with being different or contemporary. "Can
we use a guitar in the sanctuary?" "Should coffee be served
in the services?" "Should the preacher sit on a stool rather
than stand behind a box?" But it does suggest that renewal
is synonymous with a God-given vision of reality that will
shape a new model for the church. Models are created out
of our often-hidden priorities of ministry. They are institutional efforts to answer the question, "What do the
people of this community need?" Renewal can be effectively stopped if we seek to answer the question by how we
see those felt needs instead of asking the people themselves.

5. *All models are adaptational.* If our vision of ministry is
threatened by conflict or cultural dissonance, the model
seeks to accommodate the dissonance rather than reor-
ganize itself to face the new conflict. Given enough ac-
commodation, a new model may emerge. But ordinarily
each model is characterized by a high degree of conservatism. Try changing the time of the morning service to
noon or switching the hours of Sunday school and morning
worship. Many of our traditional meeting times were
structured to meet the needs of a rural community and the
farm chores that had to be finished before we could go to
morning worship. Now we are urban but our times of
meeting remain oriented to milking cows.

One of the largest fellowships in the Philadelphia area is
the Living Word Fellowship, a charismatic assembly. In
1969 the son of its long-term pastor asked for change. He
proposed that the church meet for common worship only
once a week and that a network of house churches be set up
for fellowship and what we now call "body life." The
church board decided to try his suggestion. Within a few
weeks, the church lost almost all its membership; fewer
than ten families were willing to try the new experiment.
Why? Were the members who left any the less filled with
the Spirit after that change than before? I doubt it. They
were simply threatened by the radicalness of the shift

suggested. It was too large a change to assimilate without destroying their old model. However, the church now has eight hundred attending that one celebration service a week and has given birth to another fellowship, almost equal in size. If the church board would now decide to return to the old order, there would probably be the same rebellion as there was in 1969. Models are intrinsically conservative.

How Do You Change a Model?—Rejuvenation

Given the facts of our existing models, how can change be effected that will invigorate and rejuvenate our churches? How do we work for change that exhibits faith and not faddism?

Charles Kraft of Fuller Theological Seminary warns us that before we can bring about significant change in a culture we must recognize two facts. First, such change must begin with a change in the world view of that culture. A culture's world view is its control box. Change the world view and you begin the transformation of the culture. Second, any disequilibrium at the center of a culture exhibits its effects strongly throughout the culture. Witness the effects of the white culture on that of the American Indian tribes and the identity struggle of the American black in a white-dominated society. Effective change takes place when the change agents do two things. They must be aware of the patterns and processes of the culture in which they work and they must work with or in terms of these patterns and processes to bring about the changes they seek.

What does all of this mean when it comes to models of ministry for today? We must recognize that our existing models are not simply constructed out of biblical data. Behind them, and often hidden even from those who create them, is a world view shaped by cultural leftovers. Church models, in a real sense, are microinstruments of our micro-world views. To change the model we must change the world view that underlies it. And we must make the change without creating disequilibrium at the center.

Evangelism: Doing Justice and Preaching Grace

Change must not be threatening. Where do we begin? Let me make four suggestions.

1. The change agent must seek to understand the cultural element that he thinks ought to be changed from the point of view of the people. Don Richardson relates in his book *Peace Child* how he ministered among the Sawi of Irian Jaya. He learned the language and finally, in one of their manhuts, began to share the gospel. There was almost total disinterest until he began to relate the story of Jesus' betrayal by Judas. Suddenly the men came alive with excitement. But their excitement and approval was over Judas, not Jesus. Richardson was dumbfounded. Then he realized that their understanding of the gospel was being affected by their world view. In the Sawi culture, betrayal was regarded as one of the highest ethical values. Their world view made Judas, not Jesus, the hero of the gospel. How could he share the gospel with them? Their world view filtered the gospel until it was not the gospel. Richardson did not assault this value system; he began to look for a way of evangelizing that would use this cultural element with the least amount of disequilibrium. He found his answer with the Sawi concept of the "peace child." He observed that a brutal war was stopped when a child of one of the two opposing tribes was surrendered to the other. The child would be brought up in the other tribe. As long as the child lived, there would be peace. Richardson now preached Jesus as God's Peace Child. To a world at war with God and itself Jesus was given by God as His Peace Child. Only this peace was not temporary. Jesus was God's eternal Son, and God's peace was eternal. This was the beginning of the gospel breakthrough into that culture. The gospel was used to answer human felt needs in the community in a nonthreatening way.

Our church models must be changed in the same way. You cannot make what Lyle Schaller calls a "Saturday Evening Post church" into a "body life church" overnight. The triumphalist myth that basks in the good old days of fixed neighborhoods, the affluency myth that looks with longing at the suburbs, may be part of your model's world view. So

Models: How to Change What We've Got

you begin by capitalizing on the attitude of that world view toward the church neighborhood. For example, how will a rural church begin its ministry to the poor? A rural church begins with a specialized ministry to the migrant workers who are there for about six or seven weeks every summer. Or what can a suburban church do? A suburban church discovers through study that a large percentage of widows are living in a three-block-by-six-block area immediately south of their building. A study of the age demographics indicates that that percentage will rise. How can we share the gospel with lonely people who need companionship, the newly widowed after their supportive friends have begun to disappear in the weeks following the funeral? A church with a large number of members involved in civic and political areas starts a house church whose mission activity will focus on bringing the gospel to bear in civic and political areas. The expertise myth is not attacked but used as the instrument of its own destruction for the sake of the gospel. In a Philadelphia suburb, a church is given a vacant lot in a heavily Italian-Roman Catholic area. The area has been very resistant to door-to-door calling and gospel sharing. You put your young people to work growing vegetables on that vacant lot. And in the fall the young people prepare huge baskets of vegetables, going from door to door with the deacons. Doors that were closed are opened, a word and deed ministry, the gospel show-and-tell, breaks down walls. In a few years that church has seen many converts from what it thought of as a resistant area.

2. The change agent must encourage a minimal number of critical changes. In the past, foreign missionaries have too often sought peripheral changes in culture and focused on them—for example, enforcing monogamy in polygamous societies and forbidding scarification in African tribes. The effect has been disastrous on missions and on the culture. The same pattern will result in seeking model change if our changes focus on the minimal or if they try a maximum number of critical changes. David Mains advises that we begin with the less threatening areas of change, areas where the congregation could be encouraged in the

103

process of slow but steady growth. We should talk about growth, not change. Most people don't like to change but they are open to growing. In connection with this, Peter Wagner comments that pastoral longevity is frequently a mark of a growing, vital church. Beware of the person who accepts a post as a stepping stone. Look for staff members and people who are open to long-term commitments.

Charles Simeon, the great Anglican evangelical, had a ministry at Cambridge that reinforces this point. He began his work at Holy Trinity Church amid intense opposition. For a decade his congregation refused to unlock the pew doors and Simeon's hearers had to stand jammed in the aisles. Opponents of the "Sims," as they were called, inscribed on a church bell, "Glory to God and damnation to enthusiasm." There was hostility on every hand at the university. But eventually a strong evangelical movement grew out of Simeon's ministry. He had no special technique. His Bible preaching, his exalting of Christ, his missionary passion, his lectures and sermons, and his Friday tea sessions of Bible study and discussion with the undergraduates reshaped his church model through a minimal number of critical changes. He influenced hundreds of young men, including Henry Martyn, who went out to England and the world.

3. The change agent aims at the opinion leaders to bring change. In any ethnic culture, these opinion leaders are not necessarily those who appear to be the ones in political or religious power in a society. Usually such people are largely preservers of the status quo or implementers of decisions made at other levels. Similarly, opinion leaders in the church are not necessarily elders or deacons. Opinion leaders in culture or church are those whose opinions are sought and followed. They are usually not easy to convince. But they can be won through love and openness and a willingness on the part of the change agent to listen and to respect their judgments.

I remember visiting a church in rural Korea some years ago. A small congregation for almost forty years, it had doubled in the last five years. I went there with a seminary

Models: How to Change What We've Got

student to find out why. We met one evening with the elders and deacons of the fellowship. I asked, "How do you explain this rapid growth?" There was a long silence. Then an elder said, "I don't really know. Maybe you should ask Deaconess Kim." Again I asked, "What are you doing now that may be different from your former ministry?" One replied, "I don't know." Another said, "I wonder if Deaconess Kim would know." I met Mrs. Kim and found my answer. She had moved into the area five years before with her husband. A dynamo of enthusiasm for the gospel, she shared herself and her faith with her neighbors. When a woman was sick, Mrs. Kim cooked the meals for the family and gossiped about Jesus. When one of the men in the village needed help, Mrs. Kim's husband was there to offer it. I had found my opinion leader in that church. And she couldn't even attend lay leader meetings!

4. Change comes more effectively if advocated by groups than if advocated simply by individuals. Anthropologists cry again and again, "Social change of any magnitude at all cannot be made by individuals" Donald McGavran has refined this into what he calls the homogeneous-unit principle. "People like to become Christians without crossing racial, linguistic, or class barriers." In terms of our problem, we could call it the church-change principle: "People change their churches not one-by-one against the stream but in groups." Church-changing leaders must have a vision of what the New Testament church should look like in their community and time. And that vision must capture more than isolated individuals. It must capture the people.

Main Street Baptist Church of Jacksonville, Florida, is a sixty-year-old church in a downtown, transitional area. A few years ago it was facing the question of moving out or staying. A key that revitalized its ministry was the challenge launched by the pastor to "claim a block for Christ." On a particular Sunday morning the pastor asked those who would be willing to serve as a "home missionary" and be responsible for ministering to a block in the community. He asked for a group commitment. Over one hundred people agreed to accept this responsibility and were assigned a block. Their task was to visit their block and learn about community needs. Then they were to look for ways of meeting those needs. Out of those visits came new challenges—street Bible classes; tutorial services for elementary children; programs for girls, adult education, and senior citizens; and new links for cooperation with social agencies. From the group commitment came new life for the church. They had determined together that the church would not only survive. It would live and grow.

Years ago, Charles Spurgeon prayed, "Give me twelve men, importunate men, lovers of souls, who fear nothing but sin and love nothing but God, and I will shake London from end to end." He needed twelve, not one, for church change. Here is one of the secrets of the small group that is being mightily used for renewal in our day. It is not only the discipline of daily or regular Bible study. It is not only the joys of praying with and for each other, of mutual admonition and encouragement. It is the discipline of doing it together—the "growth by groups" method, one-anothering in the Lord.

There is no utopian road to renewal. New models cannot replace the message of the Cross. New models of themselves will not be successful even though they may preach a God without wrath and bring people without sin into a kingdom without judgment through the ministrations of a Christ without a cross. Status quo models and revolutionary models in essence are the same. Each accepts a specific human structure as a normative display of God's kingdom. Biblical models, however, are shaped by a church on the move between the already and the not yet, by a restless church that is at home nowhere except in heaven. Out of Ur of the Chaldees, out of Egypt, out of Jerusalem, the church forsakes rest and relaxation for the constant pressure of the world in change. And the church then becomes an agent of change, not with techniques and tricks but with questions the Spirit thrusts on our churches. Do our models exhibit or inhibit the freedom of the sons of God? Do they release or repress the balm of Gilead? Do they loose our prophetic tongue or tie it up? Do they help or hinder our people from being the people of God? Through our models as our spectacles do we see the world as a garbage heap of Satan or the recyclable of God? Do our models make total depravity an obstacle to growth or an opportunity for irresistible grace? Are we willing to take risks to be the pilgrim people of Christ?

Notes

Chapter 1

[1]W. Fred Graham, "Declining Church Membership: Can Anything Be Done?" *Reformed Journal* (January 1980), p. 7.

[2]J. Russell Hale, *Who Are the Unchurched? An Exploratory Study* (Washington, D.C.: Glenmary Research Center, 1977).

[3]Berkeley Mickelsen, *Interpreting the Bible* (Grand Rapids: Eerdmans, 1963), p. 175.

[4]*The Willowbank Report: Gospel and Culture* (Wheaton, Ill.: Lausanne Committee on World Evangelization, 1978), p. 13.

[5]Carl S. Dudley, *Where Have All Our People Gone? New Choices for Old Churches* (New York: Pilgrim, 1979), p. 328.

[6]Hale, *Who Are the Unchurched?* p. 90.

[7]Dietrich Bonhoeffer, *Life Together*, trans. and with an introduction by John W. Doberstein (New York: Harper and Bros., 1954), pp. 97–99.

[8]Hale, *Who Are the Unchurched?* p. 92.

[9]Wilbert Shenk, "Missionary Congregations," *Mission-Focus* (March 1978), p. 13.

Chapter 2

[1]C. John Miller, "Reformed Evangelism Revisited" (mimeographed privately by the author, 1979), pp. 1–2.

[2]Jerald Gort, "The Contours of the Reformed Understanding of Christian Mission," *Mission-Focus* (September 1979), p. 1.

[3]Lesslie Newbigin, *The Open Secret* (Grand Rapids: Eerdmans, 1978), p. 31.

[4]Stephen Knapp, "A Preliminary Dialogue with Gutiérrez' 'A Theology of Liberation,'" in *Evangelicals and Liberation*, ed. Carl Armerding (Nutley, N.J.: Presbyterian and Reformed, 1977), p. 31.

Evangelism: Doing Justice and Preaching Grace

[5]Orlando Costas, "Conversion as a Complex Experience—A Personal Case Study," in *Gospel and Culture*, ed. John Stott and Robert Coote (Pasadena: William Carey Library, 1979), pp. 244–50.

[6]Douglas Johnson and George Cornell, *Punctured Preconceptions: What North American Christians Think About the Church* (New York: Friendship, 1972), pp. 29–30.

[7]J. Russell Hale, *Who Are the Unchurched An Exploratory Study* (Washington, D.C.: Glenmary Research Center, 1977), p. 92

[8]Johnson and Cornell, *Punctured Preconceptions*, p. 31.

[9]W. A. Visser't Hooft, "Evangelism in the Neo-Pagan Situation," *International Review of Mission* 63 (January 1974): 81–86.

[10]Hale, *Who Are the Unchurched?* p. 50.

[11]Ibid., pp. 70–71.

[12]Bruce Larson, *Dare to Live Now!* (Grand Rapids: Zondervan, 1965), p. 110.

[13]Hale, *Who Are the Unchurched?* p. 56.

[14]Ibid., pp. 56–57.

[15]Johnson and Cornell, *Punctured Preconceptions*, pp. 91–94.

[16]John Calvin, *Institutes of the Christian Religion*, vol. 1 (Philadelphia: Westminster, 1960), p. 35.

[17]Orlando Costas, "Evangelism and the Gospel of Salvation," *International Review of Mission* 63 (January 1974): 31–32.

[18]Leighton Ford, *One Way to Change the World* (New York: Harper and Row, 1970), pp. 37–38.

[19]Richard DeRidder, *The Dispersion of the People of God* (Kampen: Kok, 1971), p. 213.

[20]Leighton Ford, *The Christian Persuader* (New York: Harper and Row, 1966), p. 92.

[21]Cited by George G. Hunter III, *The Contagious Congregation: Frontiers in Evangelism and Church Growth* (Nashville: Abingdon, 1979), p. 29.

[22]Ford, *One Way to Change the World*, p. 111.

Chapter 3

[1]J. Russell Hale, *Who Are the Unchurched? An Exploratory Study* (Washington, D.C.: Glenmary Research Center, 1977), p. 81.

[2]Ibid., p. 82.

[3]Sidney Rooy, "Righteousness and Justice. Reflections on Revelation 22:11c and Amos 5:24," *Theological Fraternity Bulletin*, no. 4 (1978), pp. 7–8.

[4]G. Johannes Botterweck and Helmer Ringgren, eds., *Theological Dictionary of the Old Testament*, vol. 1 (Grand Rapids: Eerdmans, 1974), pp. 100–101.

[5]Herman Ridderbos, *The Coming of the Kingdom* (Philadelphia: Presbyterian and Reformed, 1962), p. 190.

[6]Raymond Fung, "The Forgotten Side of Evangelism," *The Other Side* (October, 1979), p. 18.

Notes

[7]Lesslie Newbigin, *The Open Secret* (Grand Rapids: Eerdmans, 1978), pp. 121–23.

[8]Philip Holtrop, "A Strange Language," *Reformed Journal* (February, 1977), pp. 9–13.

[9]David Watson, *I Believe in Evangelism* (Grand Rapids: Eerdmans, 1976), p. 59.

[10]Jim Wallis, *An Agenda for Biblical People* (New York: Harper and Row, 1976), p. 31.

[11]R. Pierce Beaver, ed., *Emerging Models of Christian Mission* (Ventnor, N.J.: Overseas Ministry Study Center, 1976), p. 114.

[12]Ibid., p. 100.

[13]George G. Hunter, *The Contagious Congregation: Frontiers in Evangelism and Church Growth* (Nashville: Abingdon, 1979), pp. 47–48.

[14]Ibid., p. 120.

[15]Donald Soper, *Aflame With Fire* (London: Epworth, 1963), p. 136.

Chapter 4

[1]Eldridge Cleaver, *Soul on Ice* (New York: Dell, 1968), p. 34.

[2]Vernon Grounds, *Evangelicalism and Social Responsibility* (Scottdale, Pa.: Herald, 1969), p. 7.

[3]Rudolf Obermüller, *Evangelism in Latin America* (London: Lutterworth, 1957), p. 25.

[4]*The Autobiography of Malcolm X* (New York: Grove, 1966), pp. 200–201.

[5]Douglas Johnson and George Cornell, *Punctured Preconceptions: What North American Christians Think About the Church* (New York: Friendship, 1972), pp. 29–30.

[6]Ibid., p. 30.

[7]J. D. Douglas, ed., *Let the Earth Hear His Voice* (Minneapolis: World Wide, 1975), p. 4.

[8]Ibid., p. 5.

[9]Orlando Costas, "Report on Thailand 80 (Consultation on World Evangelization," *TSF Bulletin*, vol. 4, no. 1 (November, 1980), p. 5.

[10]Paul M. Gingrich, "Consultation on World Evangelization: An Evaluation," *Mission Focus* (September, 1980), p. 50. Compare also: C. Peter Wagner, "COWE: A Personal Assessment," *Global Church Growth Bulletin*, vol. 18, no. 5 (September-October, 1980), pp. 56–59.

[11]John M. L. Young, "Theology of Missions: Covenant-Centered," *Christianity Today* 13 (November 22, 1968): 10–13. For a fuller exposition, consult: Harvie M. Conn, "God's Plan for Church Growth: An Overview," in *Theological Perspectives on Church Growth*, ed. Harvie M. Conn (Nutley, N.J.: Presbyterian and Reformed, 1976), pp. 1–3.

[12]Sherwood E. Wirt, *The Social Conscience of the Evangelical* (New York: Harper and Row, 1968), p. 13.

[13]Lewis Smedes, *All Things Made New* (Grand Rapids: Eerdmans, 1970), p. 69.

Evangelism: Doing Justice and Preaching Grace

[14]Geerhardus Vos, *Pauline Eschatology* (Grand Rapids: Eerdmans, 1952), p. 47.

[15]Leighton Ford, *Good News Is for Sharing* (Elgin, Ill.: David C. Cook, 1977), p. 100.

[16]Smedes, *All Things Made New,* p. 106.

Chapter 5

[1]Richard J. Mouw, *Called to Holy Worldliness* (Philadelphia: Fortress, 1980), p. 8.

[2]P. T. O'Brien, "Prayer in Luke-Acts," *Tyndale Bulletin* 24 (1973): 111–27.

[3]Ronald J. Sider, "Spirituality and Social Concern," *The Other Side,* vol. 9, no. 5 (September-October, 1973), p. 40.

[4]Joachim Jeremias, *New Testament Theology. The Proclamation of Jesus* (New York: Scribner, 1971), p. 186.

[5]Ibid., p. 198.

[6]Geerhardus Vos, *The Teaching of Jesus Concerning the Kingdom of God and the Church* (Nutley, N.J.: Presbyterian and Reformed, 1972), pp. 91–101.

[7]Sarah H. Bradford, *Scenes in the Life of Harriet Tubman* (Auburn: W. J. Moses, 1869), p. 49.

[8]Harold Carter, *The Prayer Tradition of Black People* (Valley Forge: Judson, 1976), pp. 115–16.

[9]J. Edwin Orr, *The Fervent Prayer* (Chicago: Moody, 1974), p. 179.

[10]Joachim Jeremias, *The Parables of Jesus* (New York: Scribner, 1963), p. 142.

[11]John E. Meeter, ed., *Selected Shorter Writings of Benjamin B. Warfield* (Nutley, N.J.: Presbyterian and Reformed, 1970), p. 424.

[12]For a helpful discussion of each of these points as hindrances to prayer, consult Jacques Ellul, *Prayer and Modern Man* (New York: Seabury, 1970), pp. 70–80.

[13]David F. Wells, "Prayer: Rebelling Against the Status Quo," *Christianity Today* vol. 23, no. 25 (November 2, 1979), pp. 32–34.

[14]Ibid., p. 33.

Chapter 6

[1]Dan Baumann, *All Originality Makes a Dull Church* (Santa Ana, Calif.: Vision House, 1976), p. 89.

[2]E. Stanley Jones, *Conversion* (Nashville: Abingdon, 1959), p. 180.

[3]Ted Ward, "Servants, Leaders and Tyrants" (Lecture delivered at Calvin Theological Seminary, Grand Rapids, Michigan, March 29, 1978, and mimeographed privately by the author), p. 4.

[4]David Mains, "Can My Church Be Changed?" *Eternity* (August 1978), p. 15.